PERGAMON INTERNAT
of Science, Technology, Engineei
The 1000-volume original paperback lii
industrial training and the ei
Publisher: Robert Max

NO LIMITS TO LEARNING

Other Titles of Interest

PECCEI, A.
The Human Quality

COLE, S. and LUCAS, H.
Models, Planning and Basic Needs

FELD, B. T.
A Voice Crying in the Wilderness
Essays on the Problems of Science and World Affairs

LASZLO, E.
The Inner Limits of Mankind

LASZLO, E. and BIERMAN, J.
Goals in a Global Community

    Volume 1:   Studies on the Conceptual Foundations
    Volume 2:   The International Values and Goals Studies

TÉVOÉDJRÈ, A.
Poverty: Wealth of Mankind

NO LIMITS TO LEARNING
Bridging the Human Gap

A REPORT TO THE CLUB OF ROME

JAMES W. BOTKIN

MAHDI ELMANDJRA

MIRCEA MALITZA

PERGAMON PRESS
OXFORD • NEW YORK • TORONTO • SYDNEY • PARIS • FRANKFURT

U.K.	Pergamon Press Ltd., Headington Hill Hall, Oxford OX3 0BW, England
U.S.A.	Pergamon Press Inc., Maxwell House, Fairview Park, Elmsford, New York 10523, U.S.A.
CANADA	Pergamon of Canada, Suite 104, 150 Consumers Road, Willowdale, Ontario M2J 1P9, Canada
AUSTRALIA	Pergamon Press (Aust.) Pty. Ltd., P.O. Box 544, Potts Point, N.S.W. 2011, Australia
FRANCE	Pergamon Press SARL, 24 rue des Ecoles, 75240 Paris, Cedex 05, France
FEDERAL REPUBLIC OF GERMANY	Pergamon Press GmbH, 6242 Kronberg-Taunus, Hammerweg 6, Federal Republic of Germany

First edition 1979

Reprinted 1980

British Library Cataloguing in Publication Data

Botkin, James W
No limits to learning. - (Pergamon
international library).
1. Social change 2. Learning – Social aspects
I. Title II. Elmandjra, Mahdi III. Malitza,
Mircea IV. Club of Rome
300   HM101   79-40911

ISBN 0-08-024705-9 (Hardcover)
ISBN 0-08-024704-0 (Flexicover)

Printed in Great Britain by
A. Wheaton & Co. Ltd., Exeter

Contents

v

Acknowledgements

It is not possible to list and adequately thank all of the hundreds of people who have participated in the Learning Project and its meetings, discussions, and seminars. These took place over a two year period, culminating with this *Learning Report* and its launching at a Club of Rome conference in Salzburg in June of 1979. The three co-authors are deeply indebted to all of the participants in the project — most of whom served in a volunteer capacity — for their valuable and insightful suggestions, and for the time and efforts they made on behalf of an ideal in which they believed. Any errors and imperfections in the final report are of course the responsibility solely of the authors.

The list of those who took part in the Learning Project conferences held in Salzburg, Bucharest, Madrid, Vienna, Fez, Paris, and New York will be found at the end of the book. We would like, however, to thank more particularly the following people whose cooperation and ideas have been a valuable source of guidance:

Uvais Ahamed (Sri Lanka)
Kenneth Dadzie (Ghana)
Henri Dieuzeide (France)
Ricardo Díez-Hochleitner (Spain)
Abdel Aziz Hamed El-Koussy (Egypt)
Mihnea Gheorghiu (Romania)
Hugues de Jouvenel (France)
Mohammed Kassas (Egypt)
Raoul Kneucker (Austria)

Pablo Latapí (Mexico)
Donald Lesh (USA)
Carlos Mallmann (Argentina)
Eleonora Masini (Italy)
Donald Michael (USA)
Bogdan Suchodolski (Poland)
Romesh Thapar (India)
Iba der Thiam (Senegal)
Jacques Vonèche (Switzerland)
Burns H. Weston (USA)

Each of the co-authors was aided immeasurably by teams in Bucharest, Cambridge, and Rabat, whose broad scientific research offered the foundations for many of the ideas in the report. They are especially grateful to the following team members:

> *Bucharest Team:* Silviu Guiaşu, Ileana Ionescu-Siseşti, Cătălin Mamali, Solomon Marcus, Victor Săhleanu, Adrian Vasilescu, Simona Vornicescu; and Ana-Maria Sandi, whose competent dedication and ideas played a decisive role in the work of the team.
>
> *Cambridge Team*: Brian Drayton, Ademola Ekulona, Cheryl Hollmann Keen, Sheila Lane, Hazel Pondza, David Roux, William Thompson; and James Keen whose dedication and insight were invaluable throughout the project and report.
>
> *Rabat Team*: Amina Alaoui, Amina Benchemsi, Fouad Benjelloun, Rachid Benmokhtar, Driss Bensari, Saida Elalami, Abdeljalil Lahjomri, Fatima Mernissi, Abdelwahed Zhiri; and Amina Belrhiti whose active cooperation and creativity were appreciated by all the members of the team.

The financial principle which guided the project was the self-reliance of each team, based on its own national supporters and means of financing, some of which was extremely difficult to raise. At the same time, generous support was provided by other institutions for organizing the international meetings for debates and the liaisons among the three centers of research.

In the first category are: (Bucharest Team) The National Council for Science and Technology of Romania; (Rabat Team) The Government of Morocco [Office of the Prime Minister]; and (Cambridge Team) The German Marshall Fund of the United States, John A. Harris IV, Institute for World Order, Inc., National Endowment for the Humanities [an independent agency of the U.S. Government], W. Nesbitt, and others.

In the second category are: Austrian Ministry for Science and Research, Fundación General Mediterránea, Association Internationale Futuribles, Bernard van Leer Foundation, and the Federal Government of Austria, the Governor of the Province of Salzburg, and the Mayor of the City of Salzburg.

In addition, several organizations gave generously of their facilities and support staff: Harvard Graduate School of Education (Cambridge), Association Internationale Futuribles (Paris), Fundación

General Mediterránea (Madrid), International Center for Integrative Studies (New York), Romanian Academy of Social and Political Studies (Bucharest), UNESCO Center for Higher Education (Bucharest), U.S. Association for The Club of Rome (Washington), University of Bucharest (Bucharest), University Mohamed V (Rabat), World Future Studies Federation (Rome), and the Center for Economic and Social Studies of the Third World (Mexico City).

The one person without whose personal support, commitment, and enthusiasm this report could never have been initiated or completed is Aurelio Peccei, President of The Club of Rome. His vigor, vision, and vitality are an inspiration to all of us.

June 15, 1979   James W. Botkin, *Cambridge*
                                                  Mahdi Elmandjra, *Rabat*
                                                  Mircea Malitza, *Bucharest*

Foreword

The purpose of this project is to bring to the forefront two intertwined questions which are fundamental for the survival and development of humankind.

One is whether what we call *progress* is perhaps so hectic and haphazard that world populations are utterly confused and out of step with the waves of change it causes for better or for worse. The idea implicit in this question is that, though highly advanced in other ways, modern men and women are as yet unable to grasp fully the meaning and consequences of what they are doing. Failing to understand the mutations they bring about in the natural environment and their own condition, they come to be increasingly at odds with the real world. This is the *human gap* – already large and dangerous, and yet destined almost inevitably to get much wider.

The second question, then, is whether present trends can be controlled and the gap bridged before a tragic and grotesque fate overtakes *homo sapiens*. To give a positive answer to this question, one must assume that the human being possesses still untapped resources of vision and creativity as well as moral energies which can be mobilized to bail humankind out of its predicament. This may indeed seem a far-fetched assumption, but many of us consider it perfectly valid. The average person, even when living in deprivation and obscurity, is endowed with an innate brain capacity, and hence a *learning* ability, which can be stimulated and enhanced far beyond the current relatively modest levels.

The plain truth these considerations imply is that any solutions to the human gap as well as any guarantees for the human future can be sought nowhere else but within ourselves. What is needed is for all of us to *learn* how to stir up our dormant potential and use it from now on purposefully and intelligently.

These or similar questions are by no means new. They certainly intrigued our forebearers in their simpler times. Nowadays, however, they have become vitally important because of the extraordinary challenges deriving from the thrust and peculiar nature acquired by the current version of progress. Conceived as the acme of human enterprise, progress has the mission of procuring ever more information and knowledge and ever more goods and equipment for the Earth's growing billions, so that they may have material wealth and power with which to tame Nature and to better their existence. Every human group has interpreted this as a mandate to seek as much of this progress as it can for its own good, not disdaining to outdo other human groups in the process.

For quite a while, humanity thought that in this way it had discovered an optimal pattern of steady, self-propelling development. We were all proud of a civilization highlighted by unprecedented scientific achievement, wonderful technology and a flood of mass-production which brought in their stride higher standards of life, the conquest of disease, undreamed-of travel opportunities and instant audiovisual communications.

But it eventually began to dawn on us that by the indiscriminate adoption of this pattern we were all too often paying exorbitant social or ecological costs for improvements obtained, and were even induced to neglect the virtues and values which are the foundations of a healthy society and at the same time the very salt for the quality of life. Then came the creeping doubt that for all its greatness humanity lacked wisdom.

Subsequently, in the matter of a decade or so, the causes for alarm multiplied. Symptoms revealing a precarious state of affairs began to emerge everywhere. What The Club of Rome termed *the world problematique* was hatching. Tangles of mutually reinforcing old and new problems, too complex to be apprehended by the current analytical methods and too tough to be attacked by traditional policies and strategies, were clustering together, heedless of boundaries and plaguing all nations, whether developed or developing, and whatever their political regime and societal structure. In overall terms, while apparently still advancing, humankind is now actually losing ground, and is going through a phase of cultural, spiritual and ethical, if not also existential, decline — thus turning the gap into a chasm.

Although well-nigh impossible to draw a map of this complicated web of problems or to perceive the most virulent knots, even ordinary people feel just how formidable the threat is becoming. They realize that increasing world disorder and real or feared scarcities of natural resources exacerbate political tensions and trigger military build-ups of demential proportions, stifling peaceful development; that in a polity where might is right the myth of national sovereignty but aggravates the inequalities among states, while social injustice coupled with inefficient, often corrupt institutions breeds civil violence, which readily expands internationally; that polluted and impoverished environments, besides vitiating our life, also drag the economy downwards at a time when recession and inflation already conflow into stagflation, spawning unemployment, frustration and still more tension and disorder — and so on and so forth.

There is a desperate need to break these vicious circles and set humanity on the ascent again. An entirely new enterprise is thus required, comparable to, but of a higher order than, that which set the world on the road to progress. Focusing on people themselves, this new enterprise must, in fact, as explained, aim at developing their latent, innermost capability of understanding and learning, so that the march of events can eventually be brought under control.

The immensity of the task does not need to be stressed. It should not deter us either. For one thing, there really is no other way of turning the global situation around than by improving human quality and preparedness — and this is therefore what we must do. For another thing, people throughout the world, particularly the young, fortunately begin to perceive that something of this nature has become indispensable — and this should give us enough courage not to waver.

For these reasons, this *learning* project is timely and, if successful, can become a milestone. The Club of Rome opened a cycle in 1972 with a provocative presentation of the *outer limits* which narrow our possibilities of material growth on a finite planet. It now closes it with this argumentation about the free *inner margins* which on the contrary exist within ourselves and are pregnant with the potency of unparalleled developments. The immediate objective is to involve as large a segment as possible of public opinion in reflections and debates on the extreme alternatives looming up and how by improving our individual and collective capacity for judgment and choice we can steer the human course towards favourable futures. The recognition, finally, of how much depends on us will rekindle faith in the human spirit and provide fresh inducements to renew our thoughts and actions in order to keep this spirit perennially alive. Should the older generations lag in this renaissance movement, no doubt the younger ones will lead it.

Formulation of the project was entrusted to three teams and a number of consultants representing different cultural areas and a variety of disciplines, convictions and backgrounds. The authors of this report did a good job, for it was no easy undertaking to blend together the vast gamut of approaches and opinions that were offered – this in itself being an experiment in learning, I am sure that all those who have been connected with this exercise will again learn much and be further motivated by the criticism and suggestions that these pages are no doubt going to draw from many quarters.

If I may conclude with a micro-riddle within the macro-riddle, I will just add that what we all need at this point in human evolution is to learn what it takes to learn what we should learn – and learn it.

Rome, May 1979   **Aurelio Peccei**

I

The World Problematique as a
Human Challenge

Introductory Note
Diagnosis and Prognosis of the Changed Human Condition

Humanity is entering a period of extreme alternatives. At the same time that an era of scientific and technological advancement has brought us unparalleled knowledge and power, we are witnessing the sudden emergence of a "world problematique" — an enormous tangle of problems in sectors such as energy, population and food which confront us with unexpected complexity. Unprecedented human fulfilment and ultimate catastrophe are both possible. What will actually happen, however, depends on another major — and decisive — factor: human understanding and action.

Only ten years ago, the mood was one of great expectations. Now, after a decade of global issues, it appears not only that the world situation has substantially deteriorated but also that adverse trends are steadily strengthening. Even though the techno-scientific enterprise has progressed on many fronts, its achievements are neither systematically nor globally coordinated, all too often engendering more serious problems than the ones they solve. Meanwhile, still other problems of a political, social, and psychological character keep emerging. All of these intertwine, so that the predicament of humanity becomes ever more difficult and the overall human condition continues to deteriorate.

Our reluctance to face up to unpleasant realities blurs the fact that the current general crisis will get far worse before it can eventually get better. The few existing evaluations or forecasts are narrow, fragmented, or short-term. Never is our vast assortment of resources mobilized

1

across academic disciplines and national boundaries with a view to pursuing common, global goals on a long-term basis. As a consequence, humanity is pitifully unprepared to cope with the formidable challenges, threats, and complexities on the immediate horizon.

We must come to understand at least two critical points. One is that humanity as a whole is moving rapidly towards a momentous crossroads where there will be no room for mistakes. The second is that we must break this vicious circle of increasing complexity and lagging understanding while it still is possible to exert influence and some control over our own destiny and future.

That something fundamental is wrong with our entire system is quite evident, for even now humanity is unable to assure the minima of life to all its members, to be at peace with itself, or to be in harmony with Nature. Consideration of just a few facts and trends will suffice here to document the change which has occurred in the human condition.

A major and fundamental problem is global over-population that results from an incapacity or unwillingness to combat poverty which is largely responsible for our own runaway numbers. Even if fertility is somewhat checked, the "new humanity" that will exist on the planet by the year 2000 will be equal in size to the total human population at the time of World War I. This demographic pressure is subjecting the human system to new, unbearable burdens when its condition is already weak. More than one-third of our population is living beneath the poverty line. Without eradication of poverty and ignorance, there can be little doubt that the same or greater proportion of our future children will be condemned to continue this fate. For instance, there exist no long-term plans for how to settle decently the new waves of population; yet merely to build the physical infrastructure of the human habitat required before the end of the century — houses, schools, hospitals, factories, whole cities, etc. — entails a construction job similar in scope to the one humanity has undertaken since the Middle Ages. Nor are there reliable plans or even ideas on how to provide work for the 350 million able-bodied men and women currently underemployed or unemployed, or on how to create the one billion or more new jobs which will be needed for children being born now to employ them in the next decades.

The signs of profound global malaise are also evident in the widening cleavage between the North and South. It divides the world drastically; and, short of radical measures, it will prove unbridgeable. Commanding 80% of the world's wealth and trade, 85% of world resources spent on education, over 90% of the industry and services, and nearly 100% of the institutions of research, the industrialized societies have grown to gigantic dimensions which threaten world equilibrium and impede social justice and equity.

Another symptom is each nation's frantic search for security which is leading increasingly to collective instability. The world has become an armed camp, and the arms race continues to spread from the great powers to scores of other countries, including the poorest. The nuclear overkill capability has attained absurd levels. The entire world population can now be wiped out many times over. Two-thirds of the non-nuclear countries are importing major weapons. Almost half the world's scientists are engaged in "defense" projects, and the annual military expenditure now exceeds one billion dollars a day. In 1976, the world spent 60 times as much money to equip each soldier as it spent educating each child.

Nor are we in harmony with Nature. The major problem is not, as generally thought, the depletion of non-renewable resources. Although over-exploited, these can still be found in respectable quantities in the Earth's crust and oceans. Nevertheless, some resources are becoming either physically scarce, or more expensive to extract and process, or both. Farmland and energy, for example, are in these borderline categories. Once wars were waged in quest of salt; today energy is, and tomorrow food may become, the salt of the contemporary economy. However, the so-called renewable resources face more imminent dangers; among these are rapid degradation of the world's tropical rain forests, the advance of desertification, and an accelerating extinction of animal and plant wildlife. If these trends continue, we are destined to lose drastically in terms of habitat, health, and quality of life, if not even the very capacity for survival.

This is the chain of cold facts and actual trends we are witnessing at this fateful crossroad to the future. They are of such a magnitude and nature, and their interactions so critical, that everything human is upset and made immensely more hazardous by their complexity. For nearly ten years now, we have recognized the dangers posed by the world problematique; yet the human condition continues to deteriorate and our understanding continues to lag, despite all our scientific knowledge, all our educational achievements, and all our research capabilities. Is there no hope on the horizon for a change in direction?*

After a decade of discussing global issues, small signs of a shift are evident in the debates. Most of the participants engaged in the world simulation modeling and the extensive world conferences have sensed that the dialogues were lacking a critical element. A preoccupation with the material side of the world problematique has limited their scope and effectiveness. Now a new concern has become evident – to restore the human being to the center of world issues. This suggests a move beyond regarding global issues as manifestations of physical problems in the life-support system, and towards an acceptance of the preeminent importance of the human side of these issues. This human side of the global problematique, or what is called the *human element,* encompasses both the problems caused by human vulnerabilities as well as the opportunities created by human potential. Directing attention to this human element is no less compelling a need now than was the critical necessity earlier to debate the physical, or outer, limits of a finite world. Indeed, without a new emphasis upon the human element, many of the considerations of the external life-support system quickly lose their significance.

Evidence of this new concern is apparent from several different but related perspectives. First, it has become visible in the growing disenchantment which has come to surround the *technological fix.* Skepticism now accompanies most proposals that relegate their impact on human beings to secondary importance and that rely primarily on technical breakthroughs or scientific discoveries. In food production, for example, the program known as the Green Revolution has been criticized for creating additional social, economic, and environmental problems in the course of solving food production problems. That is, the new technologies had the desired effect of raising agricultural

---

*The foregoing diagnosis is largely based upon "Mankind at the Crossroads", Aurelio Peccei, Tenth Anniversary Meeting, Academy of Lincei, Rome, July, 1978.
See also *The Human Quality,* Pergamon Press, 1977 by the same author.

yields, but they also demanded the use of far more energy-consuming cultivation techniques, including heavier applications of high-cost chemical fertilizers and pesticides. Moreover, they also tended to dispossess the poorer, less-educated peasants unable to utilize the newer methods, thereby adding to unemployment and social inequalities. This experience with the Green Revolution was a sober demonstration that comprehensive solutions cannot be provided by technology alone. In energy production, to cite another example, popular protests have increasingly disrupted or in some cases corrected plans for large-scale, centralized nuclear power plants because of possible threats to the quality of life or even human survival. The message of these protests is clear: put technology at the service of humanity, not humanity at the service of technology.

Second, this emphasis on the human element has also become apparent as the agenda of global issues expands to include topics that are more social, cultural, or political than material and physical. Non-material issues such as cultural identity, the emancipation of women, the status of children, and communication and information have outgrown their local and regional frameworks and attained the rank of global problems, joining the pioneering themes such as environment, food, energy, and population.* Unlike these initial topics which are closely identified with the conservation of that thin, fertile, and fragile layer of Earth called the biosphere, the more recent issues embrace human needs, rights, and responsibilities. The emphasis has shifted to questions of justice or injustice, hope or despair, well-being or destitution, and perceptions or misperceptions of people not only in their relations with the environment but, equally importantly, in their relationships with each other.

Third, as these changes gather momentum, the human element slowly is being incorporated into the search for new indicators and criteria for monitoring and judging the severity of global issues. Old problems are

---

* The United Nations System has been instrumental in this expansion. For instance, the U.N. designated 1979 as the "International Year of the Child" and is making designations for other years as well. And UNESCO set up, to cite one among many examples, the International Commission for the Study of Communications Problems. A first Interim Report was submitted by Commission President Sean MacBride in September, 1978, followed by an entire series of impressive studies on communications problems in modern society.

coming to be viewed in new ways. This is most obvious in the recent evolution of thinking about development. Now that the cleavage between the two worlds of the haves and have-nots has become wider, it has become clearer that development can no longer be defined in terms of economic growth alone. The concern for increasing gross national product is now matched, if not exceeded, by the importance being attached to problems of cultural identity, of distribution, and of social and human development. Nearly every developing country feels the need to extend its aspirations beyond mere economics in order to attain autonomy in cultural, social, and information areas as well, and this has become a significant factor in the dialogues on a New International Economic Order.

Thus, as a decade of global problems draws to a close, the agenda of human issues is still expanding. There is growing insistence that all global studies and explorations of future trends in society be based on broader perspectives and visions that keep an imperfect but unique quality of "humanness" at the forefront of our thinking. But how is this to be done? The ingenious models, elaborate global studies, and international conferences have brought us to a threshold which now must be crossed if we are to make headway in grasping the globality and interdependence of phenomena and people.

Overview
Learning and the Human Gap

Whoever chronicles the history of the 1970s will see clearly what we perceive only dimly now. Not only is a critical element still missing from most discussions on global problems, but the most striking analyses of the world problematique are diverting attention from a fundamental issue. What has been missing is the human element, and what is at issue is what we call the *human gap*.

The human gap is the distance between growing complexity and our capacity to cope with it. Clearly, one eternal human endeavor has been to develop additions to knowledge and improvements in action to deal with a complexity which, for most of history, derived primarily from natural phenomena. An essential difference today is that contemporary complexity is caused predominantly by human activities. We call it a *human* gap, because it is a dichotomy between a growing complexity of our own making and a lagging development of our own capacities.

Global problems, currently the chief manifestations of complexity, are first and foremost human problems. They are only secondarily attributable to natural causes. As human problems, they inherently encompass all our frailties and potentials. We are not certain whether the issues we identify are complete, correct, or correctly stated. We are still unable to properly assess and respond to the dangerously high levels of risk intrinsic to the world problematique. And it is not only our capacity to cope which is in question but also our ability or willingness to perceive, understand, and take action on present issues as well as to foresee, avert, and take responsibility for future ones.

It is a profound irony that we should be confronted with so many problems at the same time in history when humanity is at a peak of its knowledge and power. Yet to an intelligent being observing from another planet, we must appear absurd. High-energy technologies are still being developed in disregard for the dwindling global supply of petroleum and natural gas reserves and in the face of mounting public and scientific resistances to full reliance on nuclear power. Meanwhile research into more benign and abundant energy alternatives is given belated and insufficient attention. Even during, and partly spurred on by, international negotiations to limit arms, the stockpiling of destructive weapons accelerates to unprecedented levels of overkill among the superpowers and proliferates to the Third World.* Age-old discriminations and dangerous practices of domination and superiority continue to haunt a densely populated world which is unable to develop the equitable re-distribution schemes, cooperation, and moral solidarity on which survival of the human species may, for the first time in history, increasingly depend. Such absurd, occasionally stubborn, and often outmoded practices are but a few of the tell-tale signs that mark the human gap. They indicate that, while we live on a new level of risk and complexity, human understanding, actions, decisions, and values remain rooted in a world view that is no longer relevant.

Thus, whereas the "predicament of mankind" as identified by The

---

* The current strategic weapons arsenal of the world's two superpowers is estimated to comprise the equivalent of over 100,000 Hiroshima-size warheads.

Club of Rome first emphasized a global problematique deriving from the physical limits and constraints on future growth and development, now the predicament of humanity is increasingly seen as deriving from the human gap. Methodologies are being developed for explaining, analyzing, and formulating proposals to resolve some of the major material constraints of the global problematique,* but adequate counterparts are not yet being devised for dealing with the human element.

This report examines how *learning* can help to bridge the human gap. Learning, as we shall use the term, has to be understood in a broad sense that goes beyond what conventional terms like education and schooling imply. For us, learning means an approach, both to knowledge and to life, that emphasizes human initiative. It encompasses the acquisition and practice of new methodologies, new skills, new attitudes, and new values necessary to live in a world of change. Learning is the process of preparing to deal with new situations. It may occur consciously, or often unconsciously, usually from experiencing real-life situations, although simulated or imagined situations can also induce learning. Practically every individual in the world, whether schooled or not, experiences the process of learning – and probably none of us at present are learning at the levels, intensities, and speeds needed to cope with the complexities of modern life.

Distinguishing this notion of learning from schooling does not mean that this report will ignore education which is a fundamental way and a formal means to enhance learning.   However, other less formal modes such as family up-bringing, peer groups, work and play, and the communications media are significant and sometimes predominant factors in learning. Further, we shall contend that not only individuals but also groups of people learn, that organizations learn, and that even societies can be said to learn. The concept of "societal learning" is relatively new and stirs some controversy. Some contend that it is merely a metaphor that distorts the meaning of learning. Doubtless the concept of societal learning has limits, but we nonetheless shall maintain that societies can and do learn, and we shall not hesitate to cite evidence

* See for example, the first two reports to The Club of Rome: *The Limits to Growth* by D. Meadows *et al.,* Universe Books, 1972, and *Mankind at the Turning Point* by M. Mesarovic and E. Pestel, E.P. Dutton, 1974.

of learning processes at work in societies.*

The fact that inadequate contemporary learning contributes to the deteriorating human condition and a widening of the human gap cannot be ignored. Learning processes are lagging appallingly behind and are leaving both individuals and societies unprepared to meet the challenges posed by global issues. This failure of learning means that human preparedness remains underdeveloped on a worldwide scale. Learning is in this sense far more than just another global problem: its failure represents, in a fundamental way, the issue of issues in that it limits our capacity to deal with every other issue in the global problematique. These limitations are neither fixed nor absolute. Human potential is being artificially constrained and vastly underutilized — so much so that for all practical purposes there appear to be virtually no limits to learning.

Learning: Success that Turned to Sudden Failure

History shows that in the past human learning has been largely successful. Throughout its cultural evolution, humanity has adapted to its environment — successfully if often unconsciously — shaping its surroundings in ways that ensured survival of the species and that gradually increased the well-being of larger and larger numbers of its kind. Some societies thrived by developing their human learning potential, compensating for inhospitable climate, poor geographic location, or a lack of natural resources. Others, even some with great wealth and power, were too slow to learn: unresponsive to impending changes, they disappeared. But on balance, human learning processes viewed at an aggregate global level have been adequate to meet the challenges as they presented themselves.

Serious doubt must be raised as to whether conventional human

---

*To convey the sense of societal learning, an analogy may be useful. A century ago, the concepts of growth and development were applied only to individuals. Today, it has become common usage to refer to the growth and development of societies. Similarly, we may speak of societal learning capacity, and whether a society has the ability to learn quickly or slowly, effectively or ineffectively. A description of how these concepts came to be applied to societies can be found in S. Chodak, *Societal Development,* Oxford University Press, 1973.

learning processes are still adequate today. Traditionally, societies and individuals have adopted a pattern of continuous *maintenance learning* interrupted by short periods of innovation stimulated largely by the shock of external events. Maintenance learning is the acquisition of fixed outlooks, methods, and rules for dealing with known and recurring situations. It enhances our problem-solving ability for problems that are given. It is the type of learning designed to maintain an existing system or an established way of life. Maintenance learning is, and will continue to be, indispensable to the functioning and stability of every society.

But for long-term survival, particularly in times of turbulence, change, or discontinuity, another type of learning is even more essential. It is the type of learning that can bring change, renewal, restructuring, and problem reformulation — and which we shall call *innovative learning*.

Throughout history, the conventional formula used to stimulate innovative learning has been to rely on the shock of events. Sudden scarcity, emergency, adversity, and catastrophe have interrupted the flow of maintenance learning and acted — painfully but effectively — as ultimate teachers. Even up to the present moment, humanity continues to wait for events and crises that would catalyze or impose this primitive *learning by shock*. But the global problematique introduces at least one new risk — that the shock could be fatal. This possibility, however remote, reveals most clearly the crisis of conventional learning: primary reliance on maintenance learning not only is blocking the emergence of innovative learning, but it renders humanity increasingly vulnerable to shock; and under current conditions of global uncertainty, learning by shock is a formula for disaster.

Why does the pattern of learning that succeeded in the past fail in the present? What change in the human condition requires a change in human learning? The changes go much deeper than simply the possibility of annihilation of the human species through war, massive nuclear accident, sudden depletion of the ozone layer, or an irreversible "greenhouse effect". Even in cases less threatening to the survival of life itself, the reliance on reaction, crisis management, and even apparently mild shock can be self-defeating. Because global issues can have unusually long lead times, and because maintenance learning has unfortunately long lag times an important risk and cost of discouraging innovative learning is that indispensable options may not be available at the time they are needed. There is no room for mistakes inherent in learning by trial and error when the subject is for example large, centralized and costly energy installations. Learning about alternative sources of power must occur before it is forced upon us by high energy prices, petroleum scarcities, or nuclear accidents.

The advent of the global problematique also delineates the end of a period where learning could be denied to a portion of humanity without adverse effects. It is no longer practical to rely on conventional learning at a time when people are increasingly conscious of their rights and of their capacity to support — or impede — measures handed down from above. Irrespective of any consideration of the immorality of restricting learning by race, sex, culture, or nation, no way has yet been devised to generate widescale understanding, cooperation, and participation of some critical mass of the world's inhabitants in the short time period often required. Shock learning can be seen as a product of elitism, technocracy, and authoritarianism. Learning by shock often follows a period of overconfidence in solutions created solely with expert knowledge or technical competence and perpetuated beyond the conditions for which they were appropriate. Should global shock occur, many of the positive accomplishments of science and technology are likely to be discarded in a reaction against elitism and technocracy.

Moreover, because the global problematique affects all four and a half billion people grouped into more than 150 nation states and territories whose boundaries cut across a much higher number of cultures, it demands a type of learning that emphasizes value-creating more than value-conserving. The search for a global consensus on certain key values should not undermine the vital diversity of cultures and their corresponding value systems. At the same time, recognizing the claims of diverse cultures to their own identity also entails the necessity of encouraging joint responsibility for the solution of global problems.

The conventional pattern of *maintenance/shock learning* is inadequate to cope with global complexity and is likely, if unchecked, to lead to one or more of the following consequences: (a) The loss of control over events and crises will lead to extremely costly shocks, one of which could possibly be fatal. (b) The long lag times of maintenance learning virtually guarantee the sacrificing of options needed to avert a whole series of recurring crises. (c) The reliance on expertise and short time periods intrinsic to learning by shock will marginalize and alienate more and more people. (d) The incapacity quickly to reconcile value conflicts under crisis conditions will lead to the loss of human dignity and of individual fulfillment.

The net result of following any one of these paths is that humanity persistently will lag behind events and be subjected to the whims of crisis. The fundamental question that this prospect raises is whether humanity can learn to guide its own destiny, or whether events and crises will determine the human condition.

Bridging the Human Gap: What Type of Learning?

The main purpose of this report is to initiate a debate on learning and the future of humanity, centered around the concept of innovative learning and its chief features. We make no claim that this report provides a definitive statement about learning that will be applicable to all societies. Nor do we assert that innovative learning *by itself* will solve any of the pressing issues. What we do assert is that *innovative learning is a necessary means of preparing individuals and societies to act in concert in new situations,* especially those that have been, and continue to be, created by humanity itself. Innovative learning, we shall argue, is an indispensable prerequisite to resolving any of the global issues. This is not to say, however, that other actions involving political power, technology, economics, and so on will not also make instrumental contributions — although innovative learning needs to underlie and penetrate these and other actions as well. In the chapters that follow, we shall outline in more detail some conceptual and practical features of innovative learning. Here we shall only identify several fundamentals.

A primary feature of innovative learning is *anticipation,* which may best be understood by contrasting it to adaptation. Whereas adaptation suggests reactive adjustment to external pressure, anticipation implies an orientation that prepares for possible contingencies and considers long-range future alternatives. Anticipatory learning prepares people to use techniques such as forecasting, simulations, scenarios, and models. It encourages them to consider trends, to make plans, to evaluate future consequences and possible injurious side-effects of present decisions, and to recognize the global implications of local, national, and regional actions. Its aim is to shield society from the trauma of learning by shock. It emphasizes the future tense, not just the past. It employs imagination but is based on hard fact. When the gradual deterioration of the physical or social environment does not move those who should be alarmed, then anticipation either is not present or is not given sufficient priority. The essence of anticipation lies in selecting desirable events and working toward them; in averting unwanted or potentially catastrophic events; and in creating new alternatives. Through anticipatory learning, the future may enter our lives as a friend, not as a burglar.

Another primary feature of innovative learning is *participation*. One of the most significant trends of our time is the near-universal demand for participation. This demand is being felt on the international level as well as at national, regional, and local levels. Nation states, especially (but not only) those in the Third World, are demanding to participate on an equitable basis in the world decisions that affect them — particularly on policies concerning global issues. Groups of every definition are asserting themselves around the world and rejecting a marginal position or subordinated status with respect to power centers. Rural populations are aspiring to urban-like facilities; factory workers seek participation in management; students and faculties demand a voice in administering important school policy; women are demanding equality with men. It is the age of *rights*; and significantly not yet the age of *responsibilities*. An intrinsic goal of effective participation will have to be an interweaving of the demand for rights with an offer to fulfill obligations.

If participation is to be effective, it will be essential that those who hold power do not block innovative learning. Participation is more than the formal sharing of decisions; it is an attitude characterized by co-operation, dialogue, and empathy. It means not only keeping communications open but also constantly testing one's operating rules and values, retaining those that are relevant and rejecting those that have become obsolescent.

Neither anticipation nor participation are new concepts by them-

selves. What is new and vital for innovative learning is the insistence
that they be tied together. Innovative learning breaks down when either
is omitted. Without participation, for instance, anticipation often becomes futile. It is not enough that only elites or decision-makers are
anticipatory when the resolution of a global issue depends on the broad-
based support from some critical mass of people. And, participation
without anticipation can be counter-productive or misguided, leading
to paralysis (where countervailing forces preclude action to deal with
an issue), or to counteraction (where there is backlash resulting in
unintended negative consequences).

What are the purposes and values that underlie innovative learning?
Two different categories of values will be considered. First, we shall
argue that innovative learning cannot be "value free". It is in the
conscious emphasis on the role and place of values and their evolution
that the borderline between innovative and maintenance learning is
most clearly demarcated. Whereas maintenance learning tends to take
for granted those values inherent in the status quo and to disregard all
other values, innovative learning must be willing to question the most
fundamental values, purposes, and objectives of any system. For example,
in the debates about energy, it is not enough to ask how to create new
energy sources but it is necessary also to ask how scarce energy should
be conserved, to which priority uses should it be applied, and by what
values should priorities be assigned.

Second and more broadly, this report itself adopts a normative
value position. Already the complementary concepts of anticipation
and participation have been imbued with a positive value. But what are
the overall purposes and values of innovative learning and of this report?
The first and fundamental purpose is *human survival*. Survival begins
with the provision of adequate food, shelter, and health. The planetary
agenda would be full just meeting these basic human needs in the foreseeable future; yet, to ensure that these needs are adequately met,
innovative learning is essential. To put human survival in the forefront
as the first purpose of learning signifies that we are not discussing a
metaphysical issue; instead, learning has become a life-and-death
matter, and not only for people at the edge of subsistence. Even for
those more secure in material provisions, the dictum "learn or perish"
now directly confronts all societies — wealthy or poor — even though

many of their individual members may still feel insulated from this harshness. Innovative learning for those who oversee the power that can annihilate the human race has become particularly indispensable.

But "just survival" is not enough. The question is survival under what conditions? Individuals are willing to sacrifice their own survival (not to mention that of others) for ideals and causes. *Human dignity* is at the heart of the demands for participation and the great desire to contribute, and for the purposes of the report will be designated as the "beyond survival" goal. While dignity will mean different things to different people, we have taken it to mean the respect accorded to humanity as a whole, the mutual respect for individuals in culturally diverse societies, and self-respect.

The concept of learning must be raised to greater levels of visibility, just as ecology was promoted a decade earlier to high levels of prominence. But no team of scholars, however expert, and no combination of public leaders, however charismatic, can provide the final answers. What is urgently required is an open debate on whether there is need to give learning a higher priority in the discussions and actions about the world problematique, and on whether innovative learning is the kind that could help reverse the deterioration in the human condition.

Chapter II identifies and proposes a framework for innovative learning. Anticipation and participation are foremost among the concepts which comprise such a framework; for without anticipatory and participatory learning, global problems continue to intensify and the human gap continues to widen, *regardless of what other actions are undertaken.* Fundamental to these concepts are further considerations, largely neglected by maintenance learning, which include the role of widening contexts, the need to develop both autonomy and integration, and the importance of restoring values, human relations, and images as elements of learning.

Chapter III assesses the obstacles to innovative learning. Some conceptual inadequacies deriving from misinterpretations of theories in biology and cybernetics are examined; it then describes how innovative learning is blocked in practice by the misuse of power and by rigid structural impediments, both of which contribute to waste and irrelevance in many present educational systems and in society at large.

In Chapter IV, a number of suggestions are presented to illustrate the kinds of actions conducive to the development of innovative learning. Also, the chapter attempts to show how innovative learning might be an alternative to learning by shock for the possible amelioration of several selected global issues.

After some concluding remarks, we felt it useful to end the book with some of the comments made at the Club of Rome conference in Salzburg, Austria (June, 1979) by participants who examined the original manuscript of this report.

II

The Proposal — Anticipation and Participation:
A Conceptual Framework for
Innovative Learning Processes

The human challenge and historical discontinuity represented by the world problematique imply that learning also faces a discontinuity. The challenge now confronting human learning is to shift from a mode of *unconscious adaptation* to one of *conscious anticipation*; or, as suggested in the introduction, from conventional *maintenance/shock learning* to *innovative learning.*

What form of innovative learning can measure up to these challenges? To answer this question satisfactorily will undoubtedly require research and debate far beyond the scope of this project. But the need to make a start is compelling. In the pages that follow, we propose to outline several key concepts that indicate the direction and dimensions of the task ahead. These concepts, when taken together, offer a conceptual framework that can provide a basis for a type of innovative learning appropriate for engaging the complexities and dangers, as well as the needs and opportunities, of our epoch.

The Mounting Challenge of Complexity

It is possible to read the history of humanity as a sustained effort to overcome complexity through increasingly refined and effective means first of representing reality and then of acting upon it. Developments in knowledge, technology, power, organization, norms of conduct, and above all the creation of coherent mental constructs to represent the surrounding environment have resulted from the interplay between the challenge of complexity and the urge to master it. This process is nothing new. Whenever a problem has fallen outside the boundaries of some

17

tested procedure to deal with it, the situation was labelled "complex". Today, the oldest sources of complexity, namely the universe and Nature, still continue to pose a bewildering number and variety of facts and factors which astronomers, biologists, and other scientists try to render intelligible by new theories and concepts such as "black holes" or the deciphering of the genetic codes, to cite but two recent developments.

Accelerating complexity caused by human activity, is challenging societies and individuals.

There is another type of complexity of more immediate interest than that engendered by natural systems — a second-order complexity caused by human actions and man-made systems, and represented by a world of culture, civilization, and human artifacts. Contemporary societies face a sudden, menacing, intensification of this more recent complexity in virtually all fields. An accelerating tempo of change, a sheer increase in numbers and in size, deepening uncertainties, and extreme risks such as those inherent in the world problematique are integral aspects of the new complexity which signify a change in kind as well as in degree.

There are many sources of this complexity. One is our limited ability, despite the assistance of computers, to deal effectively and simultaneously with large numbers of factors. Other sources of complexity go beyond an increase in numbers, such as the imprecision of a world which is not amenable to a simple "yes and no" logic; the ambiguity of language which leaves agreed-upon international documents open to varying interpretations; the uncertainty of future events which renders obsolete the old mental habit of ignoring long-term implications; and finally the search for the globality and the whole.

This last factor is to be understood not only in the widening horizons of concern implied by "interdependence", but in the need to grasp new interconnections among phenomena and people and to develop a better capacity for synthesis. In the field of ecology, for example, we were caught methodologically unprepared to deal with the counter-intuitive behaviour of large systems whose deceptive resilience, once exceeded, can give way to discontinuity, rupture, and even catastrophe.

Two basic ways to reduce complexity can be envisaged. The first is to attempt to simplify reality. Much of the work of science is aimed at formulating simple hypotheses and creating powerful concepts to increase our understanding. This approach all too often entails the pitfall of slipping into "reductionism" where simplifying concepts are reduced to over-simplifications.

The second strategy is to "absorb" complexity by differentiating, restructuring, and improving our means to cope with it. It is this process we have in mind when we speak of learning. Through learning, individuals and societies can develop the capacity to face new situations of growing complexity. This approach harmonizes humanity with a pervasive trend in nature to progress from simple units to ever more complex configurations. With human action and societies more complex today than in the past, learning must speed up its pace to avoid lagging behind the objective processes or independent events of nature and society. It is this current shortfall, which is what we termed the human gap, that makes complexity seem overwhelming and unmanageable.

The Widening Context

As the contexts widen and multiply, and as the values that these contexts encompass grow more varied, the process of understanding becomes more difficult. Partly for this reason, many people tend to restrict the number of contexts and values they are willing to consider in regard to a given issue. The easier, although often riskier, way to cope with complexity is to fall back on reliance on old formulas. This tendency is characteristic of maintenance learning.

Interrelationships and interdependence widen the context. As contexts proliferate, and as more values are drawn in, understanding becomes more difficult.

An example will illustrate how the seemingly inexorable proliferation and widening of contexts become significant in formulating a framework for innovative learning. Take, for instance, the following sentence:

"The Sunday edition of a big newspaper printed in one million copies consumes a hundred acres of forest."

This is, of course, a piece of knowledge which can be committed to memory to be retrieved under appropriate circumstances. That is the usual procedure of most formal school learning, where memorization and rote-learning are still practiced on an incredible scale.

The sentence is also a message carrying a datum of information which can be measured by the uncertainty it helps to remove. We can test and improve the algorithms and calculations on which it is based. A linguistic approach may verify the syntactical correctness of the sentence and help suggest equivalent forms of expressing the thought. Logic may help us to concentrate on the degree of truth or falsity of the assertion and furnish some procedures to test its validity. All these approaches have their own merits.

The main issue for us, however, is whether and how the statement can enter into a process of innovative learning. The first prerequisite of innovative learning is understanding. The sentence can increase competence to undertake new forms of action only to the extent that it induces understanding; and essential to understanding is the context, which bestows meaning. In what way does the context influence understanding and contribute to meaning?

What we know with some degree of certainty is that incoming information such as that provided by the newspaper-forest statement is compared to an array of previous knowledge or, if you prefer, by the existing "schemata" of the mind. The statement triggers an inference procedure. It calls for recollection of other earlier contexts to which "newspaper" and "forest" can be related. The activation of the inference procedure in this case immediately discloses the implied danger that a growing rate of newspaper production would eventually destroy all the forests. A tension is set up between the values attributed to newspapers and those attributed to forests; and, depending on the contexts, some people will remain indifferent, others will become alarmed. Some may quote Plato on the deforestation of Ancient Greece, others will remember a forest fire.

At the individual level, innovative learning occurs only if the receiver of the message will henceforth regard a newspaper differently or look at a tree with a different eye. The statement with its calculations may be forgotten, only the meaning of it being retained. We tend to condense information, store its meaning, and rely only on its essence for future use.

At the societal level, newspapers and forests are regulated by laws, policies, institutions, and philosophies. The statement above can trigger understanding only through a learning process that entails public debate, the development of ecological concern, the emergence of attitudes critical of existing regulations, and the revision of current technological assessments. Innovative societal learning usually occurs only when a rather large series of parameters change. In this case, for example, there could be a shift towards reliance on other information media, towards reuse and recycling in the newspaper industry, towards new programs of afforestation, and the like.

The link between individual learning and societal learning should be obvious: unless individuals learn how to act about trees and newspapers, there will be no public support and initiative in society for new attitudes and actions; conversely, unless society creates relevant programs and policies (such as refuse collection for recycling or campaigns to plant trees, etc.), individual learning will have little or no impact.

But here is precisely a key issue: the link between individual and societal learning is not well established. While the learning of individuals surely forms the basis for any societal learning, relatively few individuals consciously involve themselves in the broader, and more difficult, process of societal learning. Yet as the need grows to take account of many contexts, the test of the effectiveness of individual learning is in-

Individuals are not learning as quickly as their societies must.

creasingly that of the societal response. The problem is that *individuals* are not learning as quickly, or as innovatively, as their *societies* must. What are some underlying explanations for this situation?

The search for meaning — the desire to grasp a problem, to understand its significance, and to envisage solutions — is central in the present world. One cannot make sense of the overwhelming overload of information without the selective criteria provided by meaning. One cannot avoid the non-critical acquisition of facts and the mechanical repetition of given patterns of action except through the grasping of meaning. It is the neglect of meaning when sending or receiving information, or when urging or undertaking action, that creates a risk of alienating the individual from society.

The meaning of a sentence comprises more than its degree of conformity to some agreed-upon rules. We can store in a computer the most refined grammatical rules, taken with the richest vocabulary of words, and yet the computer will fail to understand a nursery rhyme. The understanding of language is not reducible to a translation from one code to another. Philosophers have debated at length the intricate problem of meaning. Many suggest "correct use" as a distinctive determinant of meaning. But too many terms, skills, technologies, and patterns of actions are applied in an apparently correct manner, observing perfectly established rules, but with no understanding whatever. An old British story tells of an elderly railway man who, at his retirement after thirty years of irreproachable service, asks his colleagues gathered for the celebration, why it was that he had to hit the wheels with a hammer each time the train was stationed. No one knew the answer. Current sociology is now concerned with the possible emergence of a "railway hammer civilization" in which people are repeating patterns and forms of behavior without any hint of the reasons, laws, and purposes behind them.*

The role of contexts in generating meaning and understanding is highlighted by recent research — although much more research is needed before firm conclusions can be drawn — on how human memory works. Linear stage theory — according to which physical signals perceived by our senses arrive first to short-term memory, later to be deposited in a slot in long-term memory — has been superseded. New research suggests, in brief, that cognitive processes consist basically in the matching of new information inputs against appropriate mental schemata which are part of a vast number of frameworks created by past experience. Each frame or schema creates a cohesive structure from the incoming data. Our brain does not store memorized items in isolation, but keeps them in multiple copies according to the contexts associated with their arrival. These contexts will influence their content and will help in their subsequent retrieval.

*G. Friedmann calls it a "driver's civilization" in *Travail en Miettes,* Gallimard, Paris, 1956 (English translation, Heinemann, London, 1961).

As the number of these contexts grows, understanding and learning are profoundly affected. How else could the same event announced in the news produce such different reactions from various countries (or groups within a country) if not because of the differing contexts in which it is interpreted? We hear that a conflict has broken out some-where in the world. Some may remain indifferent to the news. But the response is otherwise for a generation which still has in its ears the scream of air raid sirens and recalls images of roads crowded with dis-placed people and innocent victims. The reaction of a group that has been fighting for the last decade, never knowing the rest and benefits of peace, is very different from that of a group with no first-hand experience of war.

It is, incidently, not only through real-life situations that we acquire new contexts. Television creates credible, moving, and staggering contexts for us, even for remote, fictitious, or simulated events.

Yet at a time when contexts are widening, they are systematically narrowed down into predetermined and preconceived forms both in formal schooling as well as in the theoretical approach to education in general — despite the fact that their role is decisive for understanding. There is a myth to be dispelled: the idea that real knowledge and learning may be attained only when they are "purified" of their con-texts.

The neglect of contexts im-pedes learning. Information is circulated with the pre-tension of being understood irrespective of the context.

We submit that many of the difficulties of learning today stem from the neglect of contexts. Statements, norms, values, cultural arti-facts, technology, and infor-mation are circulated or trans-ferred from one place to another, from one group to another, and from one individual to another, with the pretension that they are com-prehensible without regard for the contexts in which they were created or received. Innovative learning cannot be the mere digestion of an input, resulting in an output; nor can it be a simple additive process of connecting values to things.

In order to enhance the human capacity to act in new situations and to deal with unfamiliar events, innovative learning requires the absorption of vast collections of contexts. When contexts are restricted, the probability of shock learning increases, for shock may be conceived as a sudden event that occurs outside the known contexts. Hence one task of innovative learning is to enhance the individual's ability to find, absorb, and create new contexts — in short, to enrich the supply of contexts. If the existing supply cannot offer the required analogy to deal with new or unexpected events, then we must develop the capacity to construct suitable alternative mental frameworks.

Does this approach open the door to barren subjectivity in which truth is purely relative? If everything depends on the context, what remains of the chance to create a world consciousness to solve shared world problems?

The answer is that enrichment of contexts implies the need for a companion ability. To avoid the dangers of misleading or parochial understanding, it is essential to develop the capacity to compare different contexts and to reconcile their conflicts. Meanings are seldom private. They require intersubjective validation. It is through communication that individual contexts are confronted, shared, expanded, or changed. Hence the importance of *interaction,* which permits us to transcend individual meaning, to recognize larger shared interests, and to maintain flexibility in our storehouse of contexts.

Therefore, two capacities assume particular importance for innovative learning. On the one hand, individuals have to be able to enrich their contexts, keeping up with the rapid appearance of new situations. On the other hand, they must communicate the variety of contexts through an on-going dialogue with other individuals. The one is pointless without the other. Cultivating understanding in isolation can lead to reliance on self-defeating, quickly obsolescent, local truth; and ignoring the contexts of others usually engenders the danger of narrow-mindedness and a false sense of security.

Anticipation and Participation: The Main Features of Innovative Learning

The challenge of complexity, the poorly-established linkages between individual and societal learning, the widening of contexts, and the need both to enrich and compare contexts through dialogue and interaction are several among many factors underlying the need for and requirements of innovative learning. These requirements can be described by two key concepts which we believe constitute the main features of innovative learning — anticipation and participation.

Anticipatory Learning: Encouraging Solidarity in Time

Anticipation is the capacity to face new, possibly unprecedented, situations; it is the acid test for innovative learning processes. Anticipation is the ability to deal with the future, to foresee coming events as well as to evaluate the medium-term and long-range consequences of current decisions and actions. It requires not only learning from experience but also "experiencing" vicarious or envisioned situations. An especially important feature of anticipation is the capacity to account for unintended side effects, or "surprise effects" as some people call them.

Furthermore, anticipation is not limited simply to encouraging desirable trends and averting potentially catastrophic ones: it is also the "inventing" or creating of new alternatives where none existed before.* That is, anticipation economizes the valuable but time-consuming process of undergoing experience; it helps to ward off traumatic and costly lessons by shock. At the same time, it makes possible increasingly substantial and conscious influence over the course of the future.

Anticipation is not limited to foreseeing or choosing among the desirable trends and averting catastrophic ones: it is also the creating of new alternatives.

There is a somewhat fatalistic notion that society learns only from its day-to-day experiences, and very little if anything from these. How many lessons must history teach before we learn to live in peace? How many world wars must we suffer in order to learn to avoid new ones? It is incredible how many

* See Hazel Henderson, *Creating Alternative Futures: The End of Economics*, Berkeley Publishing Corporation, New York, 1978, and Dennis Gabor, *Inventing the Future*, Secker & Warburg, London, 1963.

people are so pessimistic as to believe that nuclear war is the only path to true disarmament. It is unbelievable how many societies simply wait for problems to worsen before seeking remedies. In non-anticipatory, adaptive learning, all we do is "react", and search for answers when it might be too late to implement solutions. We exhibit great insensitivity to small but critical signals. Under the influence of maintenance learning, those who should be alarmed are often not moved by gradual deterioration. Then when shock occurs and events roll like thunder, people finally stand up only to look for the lightning that has already struck.

Since innovative learning emphasizes preparedness to act in *new* situations, the exploration of what may happen or is likely to occur necessarily becomes one of the main pillars of the learning enterprise. At the present time, however, anticipation does not play a sufficiently important role. As individuals, we do not speak enough in the future tense; and as societies, we tend to speak only in the past tense.*

"Societal anticipation" will be one of the most important characteristics that a society of the twenty-first century can display. How difficult — but not impossible — it is to achieve this is evident, for instance, in the role of the communications media. Even when the mass media seem to be doing their duty of providing early warning, they usually are reporting on isolated episodes, without revealing global trends or processes. Newspaper items are like separate pieces of a jigsaw puzzle that alone do not convey any coherent meaning nor encourage anticipation. There is, for example, no widely understood scenario about accidental nuclear war; yet, as such weapons proliferate, accidental nuclear war ceases to be a fictitious possibility.

Individuals can learn to anticipate. What would it take to achieve "societal" anticipation?

Some would reduce anticipation to the faculty upon which it is based: imagination. Certainly anticipation involves imagination, but it is not to be confused with it. Anticipation can be as cool, prosaic, and data-based as an accountant's balance sheet. Many instances of anticipa-

---

* For an excellent analysis of why this is so and what is required of organizations and individuals to overcome this retrogressive orientation, see Donald N. Michael, *On Learning to Plan and Planning to Learn*, Jossey Bass, San Francisco, 1973.

tion are like archeological diggings: both are based on a search for hard
fact, although one projects back into time while the other projects
forward. Anticipation in the form of projections, forecasts, and scenarios
is already fundamental to future studies, but it is by no means limited
to this field. In fact, there are anticipative branches of all human
activities. In literature there is the genre of science fiction, which
popularizes the feelings and concern for the future which science has
in store. In management and long-range planning, there is a new stress
on the evolution of prospective studies. Some young people take —
and many more should be open to — an anticipatory stand almost by
definition, being willing to learn from the perspective of their whole
life spread out ahead of them.

Yet despite this flourishing resurgence of anticipatory activities,
our current conceptions and processes of learning do not seem to take
full advantage of them. Learning is not anticipatory enough either in
the general decision-making processes of society or in educational
systems. Yet to be a good educator necessarily implies that a teacher be
future-oriented. Increasingly, the best teachers are those who have
developed and can communicate a sense of the future. At present, however, there is insufficient appreciation of the world of changes on the
horizon. Look at the question of employment: it is projected that by
the year 2000, seventy percent of the professions will be new. Who knew
in 1950 what a computer program was? And now the forecasts indicate
that the number of programmers around the world is continuing to
increase dramatically. New developments are evident on every front:
not only concerning jobs, but also affecting cities and housing, energy
and travel, medicine and genetic engineering, and laws and legal institutions as well. Yet when children are encouraged to anticipate the future
in terms of drawings or written stories, most of them simply extrapolate
current trends: bigger cities, more apartments, faster travel, robots,
space platforms, more leisure instead of work, and so on. What will be
really new is usually missing. We tend to see the future in terms of the
present, and not the present in terms of the future.

Anticipation is more than the act of mental simulation. It is a pervasive
attitude. It is not a separate chapter, it colors the whole story. What is
meant by an anticipatory attitude may be seen in the following
example. One anticipates well if one takes an umbrella when rain is

likely. That is the act; but there is also a broader attitude. As individuals,
we do not (yet) influence the
rain, but we are beginning to
do so collectively through
science and technology.
Similarly, in many other
fields, we as societies and even
as individuals have begun to influence or determine events. Hence the
attitude of anticipation goes beyond the mere act of foreseeing external
events — it includes the responsibility inherent in our influence and
possible control over future events. Anticipation is therefore far more
than the measurement of probability. It is essentially the creation of
possible and desirable futures,* as well as selecting plans and actions
designed to bring them about.

Anticipation implies taking responsibility for our ability to influence — and in some cases, determine — the future.

The movement from simple projections to more sophisticated levels
can be seen in the field of modeling and simulation. Several decades
ago, the first models of future events were based solely on past trends.
They were "extrapolative" in that they inferred the course of future
developments purely on the basis of past behavior. Later, these prospective models began to take into account values attributed to certain
outcomes. Scenarios became more and more related to preferred goals.
For example, the Latin American model† developed by the Bariloche
Foundation emphasized the normative goal of meeting basic human
needs in keeping with the values of equality and equity, and the Mesa-
rovic/Pestel‡ World Integrated Model made explicit provisions for the
inclusion of subjective social and individual choices. Now the most
important test of the presence of anticipation confronts the modelers:
Can models be developed to assist in the formulation and creation of
new events which are not yet on the list of desirable and undesirable
ones? Anticipation, as a critical part of innovative learning, is inseparable
from an increased emphasis on conjectures, hypotheses, scenarios,
simulations, models, trends, plans, long-term views, and an examination

---

* The distinction between possible and desirable futures was emphasized by
Bertrand de Jouvenel.

† A. Herrera, H. D. Scolnik, *et al.*, *Catastrophe or a New Society? A Latin American
World Model*, Ottawa: International Development Research Center, 1976.

‡ M. Mesarovic and E. Pestel, *op. cit.*

of the hidden implications of our actions — both in our individual thinking and in the debates of the society at large.

Participatory Learning: Creating Solidarity in Space

Whereas anticipation encourages solidarity in time, participation creates solidarity in space. Anticipation is temporal while participation is geographic or spatial. Where anticipation is a mental activity, participation is a social one. There are many reasons why anticipation must be complemented by an additional feature, and why participation should be that complementary feature. On the one hand, it is no longer feasible to hand down decisions or ready-made solutions from above. On the other hand, there is a need for the social interaction inherent in participation, both to reconcile differing anticipations as well as to develop the harmony or consensus essential to implementing a chosen course of action. There is a near-universal demand for increased participation at all levels. More people are aware of, and are using, their capacity to obstruct rather than to support decisions reached without their concurrence, regardless of the merits of such decisions.

In proposing participation as a key feature of innovative learning, we are well aware of the many problems and implications as well as the possibilities that surround the concept. In many societies, participation as we know it is in crisis, resulting in confrontation and deadlock. In other societies, some of the most fundamental elements of participation are denied. And at the international level, evidence of both situations can be cited, depending on the circumstances. Probably no area is so essential to innovative learning as participation, and at the same time probably no greater need exists than to learn how to participate effectively.

The term participation is not new. Few words convey so powerfully the idea of the individual's aspiration to be a partner in decision-making, of the unwillingness to accept unduly limited roles, and of the desire to live life more fully. Few terms suggest so forcefully people's claim to influence both local and global decisions that shape their environment and lives, coupled with people's aspirations for equality as well as their refusal to accept marginal positions or subordinated status.

Effective participation presupposes an individual's aspiration to integrity and dignity, as well as an ability to take initiative. While the *right* to participate can be "granted", neither participation itself nor the responsibilities and obligations inherent in it can be "given" or given away. Real participation is voluntary; "compulsory" participation is likely to be counter-productive.

In many societies, participation has tended to focus on problem-solving, despite the fact that we know that many solutions engender more serious problems than the ones they solve. Effective participation, however, relies much more on developing a common understanding to a problem. Solutions then become almost self-evident, are better supported, can be more readily implemented, and are less likely to generate unwanted repercussions. The common search to understand a problem also generates less conflict, allowing more meaningful participation than jumping to proposed solutions whose originators are then put into conflictual positions, thereby impeding the subsequent implementation of any solution adopted.* Creative participation thus emphasizes problem detecting, problem perceiving, problem formulating, and common understanding, and is not restricted merely to problem solving.

Problem-solving has been overemphasized. Creative participation needs to stress identification, understanding, and re-formulation of problems.

The right to participate is integrally linked to the right to learn. Individuals learn by participating in interactions with society; and society learns from the participation of groups and individuals in its activities. One measure of the potential for innovative learning in a society is its degree of effective participation. And from a global view, the potential for innovative learning in the world system as a whole hinges on the extent of participation at international as well as national and local levels.

The amount of innovative learning in the world system hinges on the degree of effective participation at international and local levels.

* Bohdan Hawrylyshyn, Centre d'Etudes Industrielles, Geneva, in personal correspondence to the Learning Project, March, 1979.

Participation in relation to global issues necessarily implies several simultaneous levels. On the one hand, the battleground of global issues is local. It is in the rice fields and irrigation ditches, in the shortages and over-abundances of food, in the school on the corner and the initiation rites to adulthood. It is in the totality of personal and social life-patterns. Thus participation is necessarily anchored in the local setting. Yet it cannot be confined to localities. Preservation of the ecological and cultural heritage of humanity, resolution of energy and food problems, and national and international decisions about other great world issues all necessitate an understanding of the behaviour of large systems whose complexity requires far greater competence than we now possess. The need to develop greater competence and to take new initiatives is pressing. For example, during times of danger or after a natural catastrophe, nearly everyone participates. Can we not learn to participate constructively when animated by a vision of the common good rather than a vision of common danger?

Yet participation today is in crisis. At present, systems often block participation, leading to situations of deadlock. Much of today's participation could be characterized as "participation by veto". Groups large and small, appointed or self-chosen, are more skilled at blocking plans proposed by experts than they are in formulating constructive alternatives. Much participation is short-sighted, and even those with the noblest of motives may produce counter-productive results when anticipation is lacking. It is clear that the skills for effective participation must be improved and that the *right* to participate will have to be accompanied by an *obligation* to accept the responsibilities it entails.

A dilemma is embedded in the participation issue. How can the participation of people be ensured in spite of the increasing complexity of the world problematique? Participation cannot be "renounced" or restricted to experts or elites. Since global issues have local causes, all humanity participates in their creation and must therefore be part of the solution. Indeed, a person not participating in the process of solution is part of the problem. Expertise may take the form of narrow-minded technocracy rather than enlightened leadership and thus inspire substantial public distrust. Many feel that even the "experts" would benefit from broader participation.

What we mean by participatory learning can be seen by examining what happens when it is lacking, for example, in an educational system. The "cours magistral" where a teacher lectures and the pupils listen is usually characterized by the absence of participation. While the modern trend is to abolish this type of teaching, it is being replaced by a great variety of technological aids which still do not encourage participation. The student isolated with earphones in a cubicle, listening to a taped lesson; sitting in front of a computer terminal, pushing buttons marked "yes" or "no"; staring mesmerized before a TV screen — these are all images of non-participatory learning. This trend to replace one form of non-participatory learning with another is especially ironic, because educational technology, properly used, could aid greatly in freeing a teacher's time for more innovative tasks, including participatory learning. It is lamentable that innovative technologies introduced into maintenance learning structures have been diverted to performing maintenance tasks, such as rapid presentation of fixed facts that was characteristic of early attempts at programmed instruction.

Participation is practicing roles. To avoid being ascribed roles, it is necessary to be prepared to approach the widest possible range of roles. Jobs and functions change in a lifetime, and in coming years they will change more rapidly. If overly specialized training comes to dominate the outlook of an individual, it tends to impede participation, to block individual fulfilment, and to contribute to personal alienation from society. Yet no society of tomorrow can dispense with specialized professionals, whether they be surgeons, dentists, engineers, or social workers. It is essential, therefore, that innovative learning combine specialization with participation. Every surgeon, for example, should also be an active citizen. Education and training can lead to richer participation by opening a greater number of roles. The ideal in participatory education is that every pupil should have the chance to play the role of president, captain, and leader, as well as citizen, supporter, and follower, so as to experience as many different kinds of roles as possible.

While the pressures for increased participation are felt by nearly every center of decision-making, it should be noted that there are several cross-currents that lead, sometimes unintentionally, away from participation. One of these is implied in the view that leisure or "the vacation society" represents an advance in social development. Partici-

Participation and innovative learning require creative work. Leisure and a "vacation society" should not imply reduced effort.

pation is an active process and requires effort and work. To the extent that a vacation society implies relegating work to a marginal occupation, then participation could be correspondingly weakened. Innovative learning is creative effort. If we consider the eight hours per day a violinist practices, or the equal amount of time spent by a student of mathematics in solving problems, we quickly realize that success in both art and science is the result of endeavor, commitment, and tension. Leisure can, of course, be used creatively. Non-working hours may be used for cultural endeavors, for participation in community life, for adult education, and in a large variety of other ways. And the juxtaposition of leisure time with meaningful work may provide needed relaxation, recreation, and renewal. The essential point is that leisure gains its value in relation to work. When leisure becomes an end in itself, it creates a negative attitude towards work, encouraging a passivity which endangers effective participation.

Other cross-currents concern isolation and apathy. There are trends in contemporary thought which, while acknowledging the younger generations' real thirst for meaning as well as their discontent caused by some theories divorced from life, recommend "direct experiences" and the organic blending of life with natural reality in what has been called the "back-to-nature movement". This search for direct experiences can lead to the illusion that involvement with the larger systems of human relations can be neglected. Every individual is also part of society, and the notion that active withdrawal from society is possible is illusory, and leads to "intoxicating isolation".

Effective participation expands and enriches the contexts we bring to issues and thereby fosters wider understanding. It consists in the capacity to be aware of numerous contexts at once, to compare their terms of reference, and to confront their dominant conflicting values. It is not a promenade through different landscapes or a random change of scenery: it is purposeful concerted activity in many settings in order forcefully to train every means to act in different and unprecedented situations. Participation in both local and global settings entails cooperation, dialogue, communication, reciprocity, and empathy.

The Main Objectives of Innovative Learning

The overall purposes of this report, as discussed in the introduction, are survival and human dignity. The attainment of these ultimate goals, however, calls for two intermediate objectives — *autonomy* and *integration*.

Autonomy

The concept of autonomy, most often linked to individuals, also applies to societies. For both individuals and societies, autonomy means the ability to stand by one's self and to be as far as possible self-reliant and free from dependence. In recent years, autonomy for a society has also come to imply the assertion of the society's distinctive personality or cultural identity. The driving force towards societal autonomy is obvious in the history of the post-war period, during which the currents that swept away colonial bonds left more than one hundred newly independent nations. The autonomy of these and all other societies is reflected in their decision process: it is the right and capacity to decide upon and to construct a coherent system of objectives, strategies, ways and means, and alternative paths of development. Societal learning processes continually improve this activity.

For societies, autonomy implies cultural identity; for individuals, it is a key to self-fulfillment.

Autonomy as a goal of learning for individuals in the attainment of the capability to make judgments and decisions necessary to act with personal independence and freedom. An autonomous person need not wait for instructions. This does not mean that an autonomous decision-maker can ignore external constraints. All decisions have to take the "given circumstances" into account. Autonomy allows the decision-maker to account for these external constraints and to insert them into a clearer representation of reality as a basis for decision-making. Autonomy provides both a key to not being overwhelmed and a basis for self-fulfillment.

Autonomy has grown to paramount importance at a time when it is still denied to many and when new counter-trends are emerging that

erode its hard-won gains of the others. Without full respect for fundamental liberties and human rights as well as satisfaction of basic human
needs, there can be no true autonomy. Where is the autonomy for the
estimated* fifty million unemployed and three hundred million underemployed or for the young person who leaves the village because of
drought to live in an overpopulated slum?

Some counter-trends erode the basis of autonomy today. One example
is the mass conditioning carried out by the communications media.
The mass media "sell" a way and style of life with the same effectiveness
they achieve in advertising commercial products, and the effect is
beginning to reach world-wide. The mass media are one of the greatest
potential instruments for learning, but they are all too often used in a
manner that blocks learning and menaces autonomy.

Autonomy, in terms of formal education, derives from the development of critical judgment. A basic condition for improving the capacity
to master growing complexity and uncertainty is a well-developed
sense of critical judgment. The transmission of off-the-shelf knowledge,
a method characteristic of most schools, does not develop this capacity.
Most school textbooks are model illustrations of a non-critical stance.
In the natural sciences, for example, the background and limitations of
scientific discoveries are very seldom described. Texts concentrate on
presenting what we think we know, but ignore altogether what we should
know. To advance is to exercise one's autonomy — to challenge the
reasons, the implications, the long-term consequences, and the limits of
existing knowledge.

While autonomy is necessarily a goal of learning, it can only be
achieved when learning itself becomes a process of exercising autonomy.
This "point of educational autonomy" is reached when people, on
their own incentive, can continue to learn, irrespective of outside help
and assistance.†

Integration

Autonomy, by itself, runs the risk of parochialism, narrowness of

* See the International Labor Organization study by Peter Melvyn which appeared
in the July-August 1977 *International Labor Review*.

† See the interesting work by A. Herrera *et al. (op. cit.)* on the Latin American
model.

vision, and isolation. But autonomy also involves the assertion of one's right to belong to the whole, and can increase the capacity to enter into wider human relationships, to cooperate for common purposes, to make linkages with others, to understand larger systems, and to see the whole of which one is part. This is what is meant by integration.

It is false to assume that autonomy increases at the expense of integration, or vice versa. The inability to think of the two simultaneously produces harmful effects. In world affairs, it is easy to find supporters of one opposed to the other. For example, the advocates of universal and global interdependence make just such a mistake when they seek to achieve this integrative goal at the expense of autonomy; so do the proponents of autonomy when they ignore global imperatives. There are many examples of this tendency to polarize the two goals. For instance, many countries which have recently acquired their independence are often suspicious of the concept of interdependence, which they feel may conceal new forms of dependency. But interdependence and integration may be conceived of as an assertion of autonomy and not as its impairment. The situation is not unlike that of a trade contract. In a contract, the partners assume mutual obligations, establishing a form of integration. The very solidarity of the contract, however, is based upon the capacity of the parties autonomously to carry out their assumed obligations.

For societies, integration implies interdependence; for individuals, it is a key to human relations.

There is another equally important side to integration – the capacity to understand the inter-connections and inter-linkages among problems. A decade ago, few people realized how intimately energy and food problems were related. Today, far too few people are able to comprehend that even apparently separate problems can be closely inter-linked. Integration is therefore also to be conceived as including the properties of synthesis and holistic perception, which make possible "integrative thinking". Cooperation also

Global interdependence should not ignore autonomy, nor should self-reliance neglect global integration.

illustrates integration. It is astonishing how the practice of cooperation so essential to contemporary life is neglected in formal educational systems where competition is the fundamental rule. The capacity to search for and enter into new interdependencies, of being open to new forms of participation, of being challenged by the logic, norms, and interests of other systems and people, is a matter of integration. Global issues are a reminder that the future puts a premium on those qualities of integration which comprise mutual respect, self-restraint, the perception of common interests, and the capacity to renounce selfishness. Taken together, these qualities underlie global solidarity.

Restoring Values, Human Relations, and Images as Elements of Learning Processes

The elements through which all learning is mediated include language, tools, values, human relations, and images. Others could surely be added to this list, but these deserve special emphasis as the inseparable

All learning is mediated by language, tools, values, human relations, and images.

agents that enable interaction between one person and another, between individuals and the physical environment, and more generally between humanity and nature.

The present theory and practice of maintenance learning tends to elevate language at the expense of all other elements. Tools still receive some attention but are often considered a second-rate class of instruments. The others are usually left either implicit or unduly confined — values are limited to those intrinsic to the status quo, human relations are dismissed as irrelevant, and images are seldom made explicit except in the arts. A proper balance of these elements is a prerequisite for innovative learning. Especially values, human relations, and images — and tools wherever they have been down-graded — must be re-

Maintenance learning has underemphasized those elements needed for innovation — especially values, human relations, and images.

stored to their proper place in learning environments if innovative learning is to develop.

Language is considered the highest and most amazing achievement of the symbolic human mind. By "language" we include not only words but also symbols, signs, mathematical notation, and so on. There are good reasons why the preoccupation with the development of language as the chief motive force of learning is increasing. Recent research in linguistics has given a fresh impetus to our fascination with language by revealing that the grammar of natural language is endowed with a special capacity for infinite generation, based on choice and combination. Language unveils the miracle of obtaining infinite possiblilities out of a finite number of elements and rules. Humans have the ability to produce and understand messages never heard or used before. The significance of this leads far beyond language. It communicates confidence to our entire symbolic universe. The recurrent and iterative processes of language generation can be interpreted as a motive force of creativeness. The development of culture testifies to this creativeness, and is attributable in no small part to actions analogous to those mechanisms capable of generating the infinite products of human language.

Tools, among which are included all those technical instruments and machines that extend individual and societal mental and physical power, also play a central role in learning. Not only do we learn about tools, but tools help us learn. They are extensions of the body (like artificial limbs) and they can provide an extension of the mind. Without them, we could not conduct scientific research, which is dependent upon technical equipment. Great advances in knowledge are often due to technical progress, as for example the spectacular discoveries of modern biology based on the equally spectacular electron microscope.

In some societies, however, the tools for extending physical power are down-graded wherever intellectual work is taken to be superior to manual labor. Another manifestation of the lesser importance attached to tools can be seen wherever vocational education is considered apart from and inferior to a theoretical education.

Familiarity with and ability to use tools has influenced the learning of nearly all people in all ages. It would be pretentious and wrong to associate the pervasive presence of tools with modern industrial society alone. The long history of tools is attested to by cultures that still strongly reflect elements of their past. Near Varanasi, where the ancient Buddhist stupas rise, one can still see in the unchanging fields of Indian peasant families the cow-driven presses, ancient tools that still grind the cane. Nor should we believe that the skill of contemporary industrial society in manipulating modern tools means that its people are superior to those belonging to pre-industrial societies. While contemporary tools may be more powerful, the personal skills required to operate them are not necessarily more sophisticated and complex. In fact, the skillful wiring of electronic devices done in modern plants can hardly match the meaning and artistry embodied in many rural handicrafts. Yet it is undeniable that the tools and technologies of contemporary industrial societies are becoming inexorably more powerful and hence more influential in the processes of learning.

The most important among the elements of learning are *values*. Referring to values as "elements" emphasizes their instrumental role in learning, a somewhat different and more immediate orientation than citing, for example, survival and dignity as values. The occurrence of value is the borderline which separates objectivity from subjectivity, fact from judgment, what "really is" from what "ought to be", science from ethics, exact science from humanism, means from goals, and even the rational from the irrational. Scientists of our century feel uneasy towards values. There have been movements to eliminate values from positivist science* and even to eradicate them, for example, from the behaviorist concept of learning.

Values play a crucial role in decision-making. The process of making decisions is based on the capacity to assess preferences, to trade off advantages and disadvantages, and to examine the future consequences of present decisions. If values did not exist or were ignored, we could not deliberately choose between one course of action and another. Politics would be impossible without values, and so would objectives, programs, and strategies.

What is important is to recognize the existence of a multiple and flexible system of values that is under a myriad of pressures for change. It is incredible how many standards we mix in the course of several

* It is, however, fallacious to assert that scientific rationality overlooks value. The World Congress of Philosophy in Düsseldorf, 1978, discussed this problem as a main topic.

hundred situations we confront daily. While most formal models of decision are still predicated on a single axis of values, they too have come under pressure to develop new and multiple criteria. The notion of a single yardstick by which all human decisions can be measured has vanished in favor of multiple and tensional value systems.

The role of values distinguishes maintenance from innovative learning. Maintenance learning tends to ignore those values not inherent in the social or political structures it is designed to maintain, and even to keep its intrinsic values implicit and unexposed. Yet it is the tension created by the pressure to select from among multiple values that catalyzes innovative learning. This can be a dramatic and stimulating process. It is one that nearly every individual has experienced: when one's values are being challenged, one's learning comes to life. From this point of view, values can be said to be the enzymes of any innovative learning process.

Values are the enzymes of innovative learning.

Like language, tools, and values, *human relations* also contribute to learning as an important basis for the formation of contexts and as an inherent aspect of participation. Participation, for example, presupposes a human orientation, positive action, constructive behavior, responsibility, and democratic sensitivity — all of which can be developed through human relations. The connection between learning and human relations has been traced back to the very origins of human society, where the flexible human group was a source of learning and action. Many studies have shown that humans are, and always have been, social animals.*

While from an atomistic perspective individuals could be defined by their physical features, a systemic view would describe them also in terms of their social groupings. Further, this view would emphasize the simultaneity or parallelism of interactions that occur among a number of associations, at the intersection of which the individual is to be found. To put it another way, an individual is part of, and can be described by, a very large number of human relationships.

---

* See for example Richard E. Leakey, *Origins: What New Discoveries Reveal About the Emergence of Our Species and its Possible Future,* E.P. Dutton, New York, 1977.

Human relations must be included among the elements of learning because the main obstacle to individual and societal innovative learning which sterilizes meaning and robs us of enriched contexts involves human relations. The obstacle is the asymmetry of interactions imposed by unequal power relationships.

Centralization, vertical relationships, and the perpetuation of unnecessary hierarchy characterize the conventional and most frequent types of human relationships. The old feudalistic patterns where the center dominates the periphery and where communications are vertical rather than horizontal still persist in contemporary societies. Armies perpetuate this pattern in all societies.

Centralization and unnecessary hierarchy tend to confine innovative learning.

This pattern is visible in industrial countries and especially in many developing countries where the state is managed by a few with only an outward appearance of democracy. There is a compelling need for decentralization in order to stimulate innovative learning. The prevailing trends toward top-down relationships and toward centralization are likely, if they continue, to suppress experimentation and variety by imposing ready-made solutions and contexts. What is needed in this period of transition are ways to "de-couple" the learning processes and structures from the conventional confines of unnecessary hierarchy.*

No less important as an element of learning, *images* have been underemphasized by societies and sciences bent on rational speculations and inferences deriving from operational laws. Images have been side-lined to a special and different role – that of guiding intuition which finds its expression primarily in the arts. An unfortunate dichotomy has been created between deduction, analysis, succession, objectivity, and abstraction on the one hand, and induction, synthesis, simultaneity, subjectivity, and holism on the other. But we cannot underestimate the advantages images have for

Images, with their integrative power and instant recall, have been underestimated as components of learning.

---

* Romesh Thapar (India) and Abdel Aziz Hamed El-Koussy (Egypt) in personal correspondence to the Learning Project, March, 1979.

global perception and instant access. Images precede words. It is not only children who "think in images" before using language. During their interactions, adults unreel whole films of images at a rate and in quantities that far surpass their rational discourse. In the processes of interaction and cognition, the human mind uses images which are basic to reasoning. Those working in the field of artificial intelligence, for example, are not so amazed by the deductive acquisition of analytically correct propositions, for that can be imitated by computers. But they are fascinated by the power of images in the operation of our intelligence, for this power cannot yet be imitated by computers. Such researchers consider images to be symbols which, due to their evocative properties, make induction possible. That is, images generate operations at the core of our intelligence by which we produce a general proposition on the basis of a limited number of particular ones.

Images also generate insight. They often follow upon hard conceptual thinking and calculations, unexpectedly revealing solutions and scientific discoveries.

While images may be thought to pertain to individuals and to the inner, private life, they also exist at the societal level. Kenneth Boulding in his book *The Image,** for example, has emphasized the role of social images as structures of subjective knowledge that involve individuals, organizations, and even societies in both private and public purposes. The fact that collective images exist — and that perceptions can be shared — links societal to individual learning. It is the down-playing of images in maintenance learning that tends to blur these interconnections.

Distinguishing Innovative from Maintenance Learning

Life encompasses innumerable routines — reading and writing, using tools and crafts, riding a bicycle and driving a car, harnessing animals and handling electronic devices, applying basic norms of individual conduct and social behavior, and so on. All are guided by rules, all of which must be learned where needed. This type of learning consists in assimilating as quickly as possible time-honored procedures developed

* Kenneth Boulding, *The Image: Knowledge in Life and Society,* University of Michigan Press, Ann Arbor, Michigan, 1956.

slowly but surely for given and recurrent "problems". The response to any such problem starts by making simplifications — the process is to define, select, and isolate a situation from a larger maze of interrelationships. This is the classical approach of science. It is also a description of maintenance learning, which is a process of problem solving* based on bounded plans and agreed-upon procedures, with well-defined goals and tasks.

Maintenance learning is essential, but insufficient. It is indispensable in closed situations where assumptions remain fixed. The meaning derived from such learning easily assumes an inner coherence. The values underlying it are given and granted. It is primarily analytical and rule-based. But it falters in "border situations". For example, when driving a car, maintenance learning teaches what to do when the traffic light turns red or green. It falters, however, when a power shortage blacks out the light altogether.

Innovative learning is problem formulating and clustering. Its main attributes are integration, synthesis, and the broadening of horizons. It operates in open situations or open systems. Its meaning derives from dissonance among contexts. It leads to critical questioning of conventional assumptions behind traditional thoughts and actions, focusing on necessary changes. Its values are not constant, but rather shifting. Innovative learning advances our thinking by reconstructing wholes, not by fragmenting reality.

No global issue today falls in the closed area of a single science or under the heading of one self-contained problem. In these situations, the task for learning is not limited to problem-solving but must commence by defining a proper cluster of problems. Consider, for example, what is called "the energy problem". It is not scarcity alone which propels the search for new sources of energy, but a vast array of factors that includes economic and political considerations, industrialization, urbanization, life styles, environmental pollution, food production and distribution, depletion of natural resources, militarization, exploitation of the oceans, and the role of science and technology. The multi-disciplinary nature of the energy situation is indicated by the plethora of experts concerned — from social scientists and engineers to architects, urbanists and transportation planners. And its transdisci-

* See Russell Ackoff, *The Art of Problem Solving*, Wiley, New York, 1978.

plinary character is attested to by the increasingly important and influential voice of consumers of energy.

Another difference of approach between maintenance and innovative learning is more subtle but no less important. Maintenance learning typically creates solutions whose validity is ascertained by the scientific or administrative authority which originated them. Adoption comes first, public understanding, assimilation and acceptance come afterwards. A key premise for innovative learning is that proposed solutions are judged prior to their adoption. They acquire values and meaning through a process of integration within larger social contexts that is equal in importance to the process of confirming or refuting their technical feasibility. Thus a key aim of innovative learning is to enlarge the range of options within sufficient time for sound decision-making processes. Without such innovative learning, humanity is likely to rely solely on reactive learning, making new shocks inevitable.

III

Obstacles — Contrasts and Constraints to Innovative Learning

The theory and practice of maintenance learning are pervasive. From antiquity to modern times, societies have developed many conceptions of learning and have designed a variety of institutions to promote the learning of fixed rules to deal with known and recurring situations. Only after periods of crisis, discontinuity, or shock did these undergo changes in kind.

Whether the conceptual and institutional designs were grand or meagre (in keeping with the imagination and resources of the particular society), they had a common purpose: to bolster and develop the skills, information, and knowledge needed to maintain the society, a function indispensable to the stability on which progress was seen to depend. The characteristics of maintenance learning, however, cannot be readily transformed to meet the requirements of another type of learning needed for self-renewal, for transformation, or for coping with unprecedented situations.

Societies have tended to wait for crisis to stimulate innovative learning.

Historically, it was the interruptions brought by the intervention of events or crises that stimulated what we have termed innovative learning. Hard lessons were administered by reality. The threat or occurrence of famine taught people to create food reserves; the scourge of disease stimulated a spectacular series of medical discoveries; war imposed in its wake conflict-preventing and peace-preserving schemes — all too often ineffective. The Second World War and especially the development of nuclear weapons mark a watershed in the history of learning by shock. For the first time, humanity caught a glimpse of the ultimate warning: the shock can be fatal. Yet in the last thirty years, there have been more wars than in any other comparable period of history, although not an all-out nuclear war.

Reliance on learning by shock has high risks: some global processes may be irreversible, valuable options may be lost, and the shock may be fatal.

The slow recognition that learning by shock can be fatal to the human species is but one in a growing list of reasons why the reliance on learning through crises is no longer an acceptable procedure for coping with global issues and ensuring the well-being of the world's population. Another reason, of which people are just becoming aware, is that some global processes may be irreversible. Demonstrable by simulation and mathematically describable by catastrophe theory, permanent damage to the atmosphere or oceans has become a possibility too risky to dismiss, no matter how remote the threat.

At the same time that humanity's protracted experience with shock has entered this new period of potential danger and irreversible error, a widespread demand for participation is growing. At a time when complexity is increasing and the pace of change accelerating, fewer and fewer people seem to possess the knowledge, skills, and intellectual preparedness to participate constructively.

A sense of encroaching crisis is abroad throughout the contemporary landscape of learning. Decision-makers, educators, and people at large sense that something is wrong or neglected. Progress is being impeded or blocked in both the overall understanding of issues as well as in the changes in educational structures needed to enhance such understanding and facilitate action. At a time when humanity should be up-dating and going beyond maintenance learning, it instead is clinging to out-moded concepts and practices.

In this chapter, we first examine some conceptions of learning whose interpretations in the shared public image of them are especially compatible with maintenance learning and opposed to innovative learning; then we assess some of the practical obstacles to the counteracting of learning by shock and to the development of anticipatory and participatory learning.

Contrasts to Anticipation and Participation: Some Learning Concepts and Their Implications

Adaptation versus Anticipation

Learning can be interpreted as "the process of adapting to changing circumstances."* Adaptive learning occupies a central position in the general public image and conception of learning, and its importance is growing as the science of biology, where the concept of adaptation originated, increases in importance and influence. But the view of learning as adaptation has its shortcomings. In contrast to anticipatory learning, adaptive learning de-emphasizes human initiative. It implies a passive adjustment to external pressures. An understanding of this pitfall inherent in adaptive learning is essential precisely because the spectacular discoveries of biology are bound to strengthen the public acceptance of the adaptive definition of learning, even though biologists may take great care to correct misinterpretations and to apply adaptation to processes in nature rather than to individual or societal learning.

Adaptation emphasizes biological adjustment to given changes; anticipation stresses the intellectual capacity to initiate change.

Biological concepts are today being appropriated as explanatory models for a whole world of human affairs, replacing the earlier mechanistic models borrowed over the past century from the positivistic, "exact" sciences such as physics. As the biologist, C. D. Waddington, put it, "Biology, the Cinderella of the natural sciences, wants to take over from her elder sister Physics in providing a framework for understanding human phenomena." Considering the popular and sometimes controversial fascination with discoveries in fields such as genetics, and given the human sympathy for work that identifies similarities and commonalities among humans, animals, and nature, it is easy to infer why biology is increasingly influencing the way we perceive and explain the world.

For instance, some considered it possible to describe the evolution of species in terms of a process of adaptive learning. The success of

* Frank George, *Models of Thinking,* Allen & Unwin Ltd., London, 1970.

survival and the penalty of extinction could be counted as lessons learned or missed. Of the two billion species which at different times existed on earth, only two million are still alive today. Darwin's principles are now commonly accepted. The world is not static — everything living is involved in a process of gradual change. The motor of this change is natural selection. The same selection processes by which changes in anatomical or morphological traits occur can be extended and said to apply to the behavior of individuals or societies also.* Those who have behavioral or structural characteristics best suited to coping with the challenges of the environment and to adapt to its changes stand better chances of survival.

However, with the development of language, the human species has separated itself from the animal world. The human existence is based on two systems of information — the genetic system, shared by all other organisms, and a unique intellectual system. While all other creatures are forced to permanently adapt themselves genetically (i.e., by trial and error) to the changing environment, humanity has begun to adapt the outside world to its own needs. By creating societies, individuals are gradually freeing themselves (through food production, medicine, technology, etc.) from the threats of nature. The laws of biological evolution are no longer applicable to humanity's self-made problems. "Adaptation" in the biological sense *follows* the changes of the environment and hence offers no solution, since it is *homo sapiens* who is *creating* the changes. Adaptive learning thus leads to a vicious circle.†

Learning as adaptation implies that human beings can only react to follow new changes in a given environment, hurrying to catch up with uncontrollable mutations, having no power to forestall or even influence them. To be adaptable, i.e., to be able to change in response to changing circumstances, implies submitting to these circumstances and even succumbing to them. It is this reactive aspect intrinsic to adaptive learning that contrasts so markedly with anticipation.

Similarly, the classical interpretation of learning as a "change in

---

* See for example, Konrad Lorenz, *Behind the Mirror: A Search for a Natural History of Human Knowledge,* Harcourt Brace, 1977; or B. F. Skinner, *Beyond Freedom and Dignity,* Bantam Books, 1971.

† This paragraph is based on Carsten Bresch (Federal Republic of Germany) in personal communication to the Learning Project (June, 1979).

the pattern of behavior on the basis of *past* experience"* is too restrictive for innovative learning. Why not learn from the future as well?
Anticipatory learning can reveal, through simulations and scenarios, a wide class of possible but future events which can and do influence not only changes in behavior, which are observable, but also changes in preparation and purpose, which may exist whether immediately observable or not.

In the context of global issues, learning from the future is even more important than learning from the past.

In both of these conceptions of learning, "environmental change" and "past experience" are seen as the motive force of learning. Anticipatory learning, however, focuses on human initiative and on our capacity to influence events, environments, and experiences that are not yet inevitable or irreversible.

Automata and Non-participation

"Automata", the intelligent machines that have captured popular imagination in the wake of progress in computer sciences and cybernetics, are often said to learn. The process by which a simple thermostat maintains a constant temperature, or by which the body keeps a homeostatic balance in the chemistry of the blood, is based on feedback, the same mechanism that is fundamental to the notion of learning in automata. This simple but extremely important form of learning as "self-regulation" is an excellent example of maintenance learning. It aims at keeping some performances constant despite perturbing variations in the environment. In situations of instability, feedback provides the information needed for corrective action and for restoring stability. All existing systems, whether technical or social, are faced with the same basic problem – how to weave through seemingly random variations of the environment so that functions and performances are maintained and a stable state is reachable.

---

* Norbert Wiener, *Cybernetics: On Control & Communication in the Animal and the Machine*, MIT Press, Cambridge, Mass., 1961; *The Human Use of Human Beings: Cybernetics and Society*, Houghton Mifflin, Boston, 1950.

The pronounced demarcation between the learning of machines and human beings is most clearly visible in the contrast between cybernetic learning and participatory learning. The contrast is not only the obvious fact that automata do not participate; it is also that the role of and emphasis on values is inherently different. Participatory learning emphasizes value innovation. While automata can certainly act "purposively", they do so only in the sense of proceeding toward a given goal envisaged by the programmer. The computer programs that drive the learning of machines are neither value-free nor value-neutral.

What separates the learning by machines and humans is the role of values.

They do, however, tend to incorporate the preconceived values of the system designer, often freezing them implicitly into the design. In cases where values are treated as variable, they are frequently relegated to the same level as mere facts. A program can measure values against a given scale, but it cannot create and choose new ones.

The spectacular advance in computers is in full swing. Never has a machine developed so fast, influencing the production, communication, and even organization of society, at the same time as providing our thinking with an ingenious and valuable aid. Inexpensive computers in pocket size will become everyone's tacit companions, introduced early in school and maintaining a relationship throughout the rest of life. Thus, after an initial stage of imitating simple forms of human learning, now computers are returning as instructors, either in the form of computer assisted instruction or of metaphoric models that explain the brain as a neurophysiological information processor. The overall penetration of computers in the next decades compels us to look further for hidden differences concealed beneath the conspicuous similarities with human intelligence so as to avoid the superficial comparisons that could distort our conceptions of learning.

Another pitfall of cybernetic learning is its emphasis on problem-solving. While the progress is amazing in the way computers can be made to learn, they always do so from a given set. The "given set" is for cybernetics what the "given environment" is for biology. Problem-solving is for computers what adaptation is for evolution. Some consider that problem-solving is the highest form of learning even for humans. This view is too limiting, for prior to and underlying the problem-solving type of learning, there must be a process of problem-perceiving, defining, and formulating. If a problem is not first detected and understood, it can hardly be properly handled.

When computer programs acquire the capacity to modify themselves, cybernetics would appear to enter a new realm of intelligence. The branch of computer sciences known as artificial intelligence has developed extensively since the days of the first cybernetic machines such as the electronic tortoise which could discern its way to recharge its own batteries. An astonishing variety of new types of adaptive and intelligent learning machines now exists. These developments constitute examples of a primary aim of cybernetic machines – to simulate as closely as possible the human faculty of intelligence, especially its learning abilities. For instance, there now exist chess-playing computers able to improve and enrich their own programs by devising new strategies that are sufficiently sophisticated to suffer a series of set-backs before gaining an ultimate advantage. The day a self-modifying chess program becomes a world grand master will not only create a hit in the news but will also represent a triumph for cybernetic learning.

A common misinterpretation of such developments is represented by the image of the human brain and learning as nothing more than a data or information processor. This view is far too restrictive. It should not be overlooked that the entire theory of information is based on a single criterion – the reduction of uncertainty – from which the human significance of a message is missing. The procedures by which information is measured can calculate this reduction of uncertainty – as for instance the tossing of a coin (the basic experiment with two outcomes of equal probability) reduced the uncertainty of whether an event will come out one way or another. We can measure this information, but we cannot state its significance or value. Thus a misapplication of information theory to human affairs fails to encompass properly the value element which humans attach to any information and which is a basic ingredient that leads them to choose, to decide, and to act.

The distance between cybernetic and human learning is measured by the step from maintenance to innovation.

Thus, even while forming an increasingly intrinsic part of the human environment in a close "man-machine symbiosis", "intelligent machines" have their limitations. These are to be stressed, not to discourage enthusiastic efforts to improve computers, but to avoid the wholesale adoption of their peculiar way of learning and the complete displacement of the specific and special ways of human learning. The difference is measured by the step from value-conserving to value-innovating, from self-regulation in automata to participation by people, and from maintenance to innovation.

An Assessment of Some Practical Constraints: Why Innovative Learning Is Blocked

Among many obstacles that impede the emergence of innovative learning, two are of particular importance — the *misuse of power* and the existence of *structural impediments.* They lead to *irrelevance* and *waste,* whose presence and extent reflect the seriousness of the misuse of power and of structural impediments.* While many institutions seem to be blocking innovative learning, there are a few emerging cases of anticipatory and participatory learning which may be forerunners instrumental in developing a new learning perspective. These are noted at the conclusion of this chapter.

The greatest obstacles to innovative learning: the misuse of power and structural impediments.

Concentrated power and its misuse are today the greatest obstacles to learning for survival and dignity. Long a fascination of history, the use and misuse of power has taken on an unprecedented significance in contemporary global affairs. It is at once the primary cause of and a potential aid in dealing with the human gap. Indeed, in many instances, the dimensions of the gap may be said to reflect the incongruity between power and wisdom, and between the unimaginable potential of contemporary society for creative action and the *lack of political will* that fosters paralysis and inaction. Why is it that the immense power comprised by science, technology, education, knowledge, information, and communication cannot be more effectively brought to bear on improving societal learning? Why have today's educational systems, which are larger and more advanced than

Structural impediments are discussed below. See pages 60–67.

at any other time in history, failed to respond to the challenge of global issues, thereby contributing to our lack of preparedness to live harmoniously in an interdependent world?

It is not possible in this short report to analyze or mention all the various forms of power – political, economic, social, cultural, and military, etc. Two examples have been chosen to illustrate how power intervenes in the context of learning. The first one deals with the broad societal level, showing how the arms race increasingly contributes to the blockage of learning processes. The second is at the individual level, showing how the mass media could enhance learning, but how their present misuse often impedes it.

The Arms Race as an Obstacle to Innovative Learning

The arms race bears significantly on societal learning capacity and performance. Recent, rapid proliferation of weapons of mass destruction has substantially increased the risk of having to learn by shock, and correspondingly diminished the opportunities to develop innovative learning. The escalation in the global arms race is clear from the data. The stockpiling of weapons by the superpowers has reached overkill proportions of absurd dimensions. U.S. and Soviet nuclear bomb inventories, already sufficient to destroy every city seven times over, are still growing. The rapid military growth and stockpiling of conventional weapons in the developing countries adds a proliferation dimension that is now almost out of control. In what ways do the arms race and these trends toward escalation and proliferation have an impact on learning?

First and most obvious is that the immobilization of resources, both intellectual as well as financial, deprives the social system of an important source of innovation, problem-solving, and self-renewal. In the critical area of research and development (R & D), over half a million scientists and engineers – nearly half the world's total – are engaged in weapons research. At a rate of $30 billion per year, military R & D

Nearly half of the world's scientists are engaged in military R & D.

consumes more public funds than all the research on education, health, energy, and food combined. Not only are these resources denied to institutions such as universities, research organizations, and schools, but they are also lost to all other institutions of society outside the military sector. Basic research into the problems, for example, of energy and food, or of poverty and development, is being short-changed.

Against the backdrop of a world entangled in common global issues, yet divided between poverty and affluence, we witness an increasing refinement of instruments of destruction such as the cruise missile. The cruise missile embodies a great concentration of human ingenuity, intelligence, engineering skill, and financial resources. Capable of following ground contours by map, of modifying its course, and of pinpointing its target 1500 miles distant with an accuracy measured in distances less than its own length, this weapon represents the height of perfection of technical intelligence and precision. But, in light of the needs of modern society, it is also the height of aberration. There is no doubt that, for the foreseeable future, there will be a need for trade-offs and balances between military and other sectors of society, but the scale is currently tipped decisively and excessively toward military research to the detriment of other more pressing social needs.

The secrecy and mystique of the military inevitably infect our learning.

The arms race presents a second, more indirect but more pervasive obstacle to learning: the projection of the mystique of the military image into contemporary learning processes. One example is provided at the international level. The concern for military secrecy casts a shadow of distrust, insecurity, fear, and prejudice over the international exchange of information and experiences. This secrecy and distrust exacerbate global issues and hinder the search for solutions that must rely on confidence, cooperation, and mutual understanding among societies. For instance, when information and data about communications policies, energy plans, food reserves, or population trends cannot be discussed openly, the learning processes of both the societies and the individuals involved are clearly impeded.

Another example is more subtle. It is the appropriation of military methods and organizational style as the predominant model for attacking other problems. The image of a swift, purposeful, efficient mobilization of resources and manpower for a radical strike against poverty or hunger belies the reality of the huge, wasteful, and non-participatory machine that characterizes most military establishments. The image also is reflected in the fight against hunger, in which the hungry are all but forgotten in the logistics of mobilizing men and matériel. It is unquestionably seen in the schools where the images of battle, victory, and heroism are glorified through the emphasis on wars as landmarks in the history of humanity. The mystique of the military image has as strong a hold over our minds as its command of money and power holds over our resources.

Telecommunications: A Case of Lost Opportunities

The neglect and abuse of telecommunications is another illustration of how innovative learning is impeded. It is because the existence of a global communications network alongside the technologies of television, radio, computers, and satellites has such a great potential* for stimulating innovative learning that their neglect is so discouraging. Equally serious is the fact that the misuse of the telecommunications media contributes significantly — in some societies, predominantly† — to the preservation of the lowest form of maintenance learning. Both the neglect and the misuse of the telecommunications learning resource may be explained primarily by considerations of power. The television sector is a case that illustrates the predominance of the power of money, although it must be noted in this regard that the support of political propaganda can create the same effect as the pursuit of profits.

Rapidly becoming more of a world-wide medium than most people realize, television can reach and touch the lives of increasing millions of

---

* The combination of these technologies goes beyond mere teleprocessing (or teleinformatique) as it also includes artificial intelligence and automatic control and is now referred to as "telectronics" (or telematique). It represents a scientific revolution with enormous pedagogical implications which we have not yet even begun to perceive.

† For example, American elementary school age children on average spend fewer hours per year attending school than watching television programs which contribute marginally, if at all, to their innovative learning capacity.

Television has the potential to stimulate widespread innovative learning.

people. Its capacity to project images and stimulate new thinking on a global scale is certified by the positive example of the image of "spaceship earth" broadcast during the moon landings to over one billion people. On the local scale, a number of examples attest to the capacity of television to promote education. In the USA, children's programs such as "Sesame Street" have been so successful in stimulating early learning that at last count more than 50 other countries have incorporated many of its ideas. In Brazil, studies have indicated that television can boost educational achievement among urban poor, even in households without access to books or written materials. In Japan, television is co-ordinated with classroom work of children in school. In the Ivory Coast, a major effort is being made in the areas of educational television. But the question is not just the presence or absence of educational television, or its use as an auxiliary aid to teachers (important though these questions are). It is also the need to use television to stimulate innovative learning processes on the part of society as a whole.

As currently used, most TV induces maintenance learning of low quality.

All television, whether labelled "educational" or not, induces learning. The problem is that most television programs — especially those that are shown in many countries as part of a global flow of imports and exports — promote learning of the most stultifying maintenance type. Even the blandest "thriller" contains a statement of values and a projection of models of behavior, almost all of which are familiar stereotypes designed to appeal to the greatest number of people. The invincible heroes of cowboy movies and detective stories, the emphasis on a predominantly white-collar — and white race — world of work, and the pervasive violence are familiar hallmarks of a stereotypic view of a world that has passed or never existed.

Today's television is undeniably violent.* Some data from the USA,

* The recent Carnegie Commission on the Future of Public Broadcasting (*A Public Trust,* Bantam Books, 1979) recognized this situation by stating: "Our age is known for violence."

television capital of the world, are mind-boggling, not so much for what they imply about any one country but because they are increasingly characteristic for every country's television. Today's average American 17-year-old has seen a total of 350,000 advertisements and witnessed some 20,000 televised murders. At the same time that some change and improvement are underway in the USA – in part through alternative and community TV experiments – the legacy of violent television persists as many other countries continue to import programs that are obsolete in the U.S. market. Programs that present new situations and increase the human capacity for anticipation are still the rarest part of TV's fare. Television has become essentially a passive non-participatory device. Most programs are sedatives, not stimulants. While creative use of the technology might foster interactive, participatory learning, virtually no significant advances have been made in this direction.*

What explains this neglect and abuse of television that prevents its use to encourage innovative learning? The power that misdirects television is primarily the power of money as reflected in the rigid structure of the industry and in the special expertise required by the technology. Economic forces have combined with a capital intensive technology to produce a world-wide system that some have likened to a modern form of feudalism. A system of smaller or larger barons of the media compete to raise advertising revenues based on the purchasing power of the audiences they can command through their programming. The purpose even in broadcasting news, for example, may be more to select and gather an audience of a particular consumer profile than to provide public information. The revenues thus generated can be applied to creating more programs to attract more people to interest more advertisers. Success is measured by the number of viewers and the amount of advertising revenues. Even when high quality programs are available, these may be withheld if it is felt that their audiences might be smaller than the audiences for another program of lower quality.

Originating in the USA, and once confined to the industrial West, television and the effects of its commercialization are rapidly spreading to nearly all countries. As reported from the University of Tampere (Finland) study on the global traffic in television, many developing

---

* Exceptions: TV screens linked to specially programmed interactive mini-computers, and cable TV that permits direct and immediate public opinion polls.

"Spots" from the World of Television

● Television is the child's early window on the world. Young American viewers spend more hours in front of TV than in class.

● One billion people have seen the image of spaceship earth broadcast from the moon landings. "Sesame Street", or its derivations, has been shown in a third of the world's countries.

● In a study of 11 countries, TV viewing was found to cause decreases in sleep, conversation, social gatherings, and household care. Sixty percent of American families have changed their sleeping patterns and 55% altered their meal times due to television.

● In Buenos Aires, citizens petitioned to have street lights dimmed rather than curtail TV broadcasting.

● In Bali, Indonesia, the fascination with TV cartoons and "Mannix" has interrupted religious temple ceremonies.

● In northern Manitoba, Canada, Cree Indians use soap operas like "The Edge of Night" as models for making predictions and future decisions.

● More American houses have TV than indoor plumbing.

Selected sources: R. M. Liebert *et al., The Early Window: Effects of Television on Children and Youth,* Pergamon Press, 1973; Gerald Lesser, "Children's Television Research", lecture, October, 1978; G. Granzberg, J. Steinbring, and J. Hamer, "New Magic for Old: TV in Cree Culture", *Journal of Communication,* Autumn, 1977.

countries are actively seeking and importing Anglo-American commercial television (with or without the commercials). In Third World countries, these are seen primarily by urban viewers, although it should not be forgotten that the houses of the urban poor in shanty towns may be nearly as likely to sprout television antennas as are the homes of the wealthy. In the developed countries, the poor watch proportionally more television than the rich, and despite the deeper and more extensive poverty in developing countries, there is little reason to doubt that this pattern will repeat itself in the Third World. If the present trend continues, we can expect the largest television audience in the world to be the Third World urban poor before the end of the century.

Why are countries importing television programs that are mostly out-dated or of poor quality? The reasons are again economic. Commercial shows two or three decades old (such as "The Lone Ranger", "Tarzan", and "I Love Lucy" – favorites in the Third World as they were or still are in the USA) can be purchased at a fraction of the price it would cost to produce any program locally. Local production, as an alternative to importing foreign television, promises improvement only to the extent that it encourages creativity. In some countries, local production may lead to use of the medium for self-serving political ends which can impede learning as effectively as economic power. Thus the "new TV countries", rather than encouraging creativity and diversity in television, in most instances have simply opened new audiences to the old mediocre fare through delayed and indiscriminate imitation. What is needed here probably extends beyond participatory learning into community participation in some aspects of the management of the telecommunications technologies and their content.

What the case of television demonstrates is equally applicable to the other telecommunications technologies. In the final analysis, the obstacles and opportunities for learning derive less from the technology than from the structure and purposes of the organizational system that supports it. Many educators are properly enthusiastic about the technological capa-

The type of learning stimulated by the telecommunication technologies depends more on the structure of the industry than on the capabilities of the technology.

bilities of radio, mini-computers, and satellite communication systems. With cheap production and easy transmission, these technologies hold out the possibility of true anticipatory and participatory learning. Simulation via mini-computers is one of the finest examples of anticipatory learning. The capacity to send as well as receive radio broadcasts is a form of participatory learning particularly appropriate to the electronic age. Whether any of these technologies will in fact be used for these purposes, however, is a function of the economic and political structures and norms in which they will operate.

Structural Impediments to Innovative Learning

The examples of the arms race and of television reinforce the view that, in general, the impediments to innovative learning are deeply embedded in the structure of society. In most of the world's societies, many of the institutions, including their organizational norms and practices, are on one hand part of the cause of the crisis of learning and on the other, themselves in need of the benefits of innovative learning. The structures and institutions of society have tended to remain stable while the environment in which they operate has fundamentally changed. For example, most of the economic and political institutions of society remain predicated on the assumptions of plentiful inexpensive energy, an unlimited absorptive capacity of Nature, a supply of cheap labor (which most industrial countries must now import despite domestic unemployment), sufficient low cost capital, and favorable terms of trade. All or most of these assumptions are now invalid.

The obstacles to innovative learning are deeply embedded in the structure of society.

The process by which the institutions will change in response to new conditions is a process of societal learning whose main distinguishing feature is the ability to restructure societal institutions, not simply to fine-tune or adjust them. The question for most institutions, indeed for society itself, is whether this process will have to come through crisis and shock with typically high social costs and risk of violence, or whether it can come through a deliberately anticipatory and participatory process.*

Initiatives to restructure institutions are immediately confronted by norms of elitism and technocracy. The widespread belief that all problems are best left to experts, particularly when "expertise" implies narrow technocratic specialization, has led to social systems marked by imbalance, inequity, rigidity, and inflexibility. Two cases of how inequitable and rigid structures can block anticipatory and participatory learning are highlighted below. The first concerns the obstacles to societal learning posed by urban-rural disparities; the second focuses on some of the impediments formal education and schooling can pose for individual learning.

Urban-Rural Disparities†

The evolution of urban-rural disparities, especially in the Third World, is a measure of the inability of learning systems to cope with the vital issues of rural development. The rural communities represent the majority of the world's population; yet they are the least favored from practically every point of view, and most of all in the sector of learning. In Africa, for instance, the rate of illiteracy in rural areas, where three-quarters of the population live, is nearly triple the rate in urban areas.

The conditions of life for rural people are deteriorating rapidly. Many of them have lost their traditional self-reliance not only in areas such as food production,‡ but also in their capacity to learn by traditional means, without at the same time developing viable learning alternatives. The resulting incapacity to meet their most basic needs leaves migration toward the cities as their only outlet. Migration is usually motivated by two major factors: the search for employment and the quest for better schooling opportunities for the children.

---

* See Donald N. Michael, *The Unprepared Society: Planning for a Precarious Future,* Basic Books, New York, 1968.

† This section is mostly concerned with the urban-rural disequilibria in the developing countries. The developed countries face another but related type of disequilibrium between the urban and suburban areas.

‡ According to the FAO, average annual growth in agricultural production in Africa between 1960 and 1970 has fallen from 2.5% down to 1.3%. At this rate Africa would not be able to meet even two-thirds of its food needs by the year 2000.

Education, one of the main means for the promotion of social mobility, has frequently become subverted in the rural world into an instrument of marginalization. Those few who manage to enter a school often either leave after three or four years with little accomplished or receive training which is totally inadequate as a base for continuing their studies or which is incompatible with local needs.

The appalling conditions of rural education in many developing countries are generally known. The school itself, in many cases amounting to no more than a common room inadequate to house all the primary grades, is often too far away from where people live. The teachers are less qualified — if they are qualified at all — than those in urban areas. They are frequently unprepared for their job and unfamiliar with the socio-cultural environment. As they begin to become more effective after some experience and practice, they are often moved to the cities. The teaching facilities and materials are very rudimentary. The divorce between the curriculum and the needs of the rural community may be almost total. Communication with other communities and support from the central administration are in many cases non-existent.

Inadequate rural education both reflects and reinforces the structural disparities between urban and rural life.

Since many rural parents are illiterate and their exposure to the communications media rare, schools frequently become the most important center of formal learning; yet even the schools are severely neglected. Statistics on the financing of education in the Third World are not sufficiently refined to compare the per unit cost of training in rural and urban areas,* but we would estimate that the ratio very likely exceeds one to five.†

Education in rural areas suffers from a lack of appreciation of or commitment to rural life. It often is not only irrelevant but at times

---

* The absence of such data is in itself revealing of the weakness of the parameters used in determining financial allocations for education.

† This estimate is based on several samples taking into account school buildings, teachers' salaries, and administrative support. Most national and international educational specialists with whom it has been checked consider the estimate conservative.

even harmful, insofar as it reinforces the rigidity of the general structure of the society by increasing the disparities between rural and urban worlds. This disequilibrium impedes learning and contributes to the human gap, especially – but not only – for those who live in the rural areas. To re-establish a minimum equilibrium between the two worlds, it may be necessary to "urbanize" the rural areas in the sense of bringing basic facilities to the people rather than the people to the cities. Some way must be devised to stop a discrimination which dishonors humanity as a whole, and to enable participation which is needed for human dignity.

Global Imbalances and Local Rigidities in Schooling

Never has the identification of schooling with learning been so widely and deeply entrenched; yet concurrently, never has the rising tide of malcontent with the present institutions of schooling swelled quite so high, especially in the Third World. At the same time that societies without sufficient schools, and parents without access to schooling, are demanding a better lot for their children, other societies and parents are criticizing the prevailing systems. While we have no inclination to defend the existing concepts of school which we find excessively concerned with maintenance learning, neither can we imagine the development of widespread innovative learning without institutions. The major problem is that schools, like other institutions of society, appear in today's context as globally inequitable and locally rigid. These faults can and must be corrected. Some illustrations for reform are suggested in the next chapter; here several of the most serious international and domestic inequities and rigidities in the prevailing educational systems are described.

Formal education, predominantly oriented towards maintenance learning, directly engages one out of every six people on the planet.

Schooling, or more generally formal education, is one of the largest human undertakings on the planet. It engages directly one out of every six people in the world as students, teachers, or administrators. Over 30 million people are engaged in the profession of

The Massive Global Imbalance in Schooling

● The wealthiest quarter of the world (30 countries with 24% of the population) spends 75 times more per inhabitant on education than the least developed quarter (23 countries with 24% of the population), a ratio three times greater than their economic disparities which are 25 to 1.

● Sixty percent of the world's population receives only six percent of world expenditures on public schools.

● The USA, USSR, and Japan account for more higher education than the rest of the world put together (in terms of university expenditures, graduates, and professors).

● In half the world's countries, half the children never complete primary school. In 1980, there will still be 240 million children between 5 and 14 not attending school.

● Thirty-seven countries representing 30% of world population possess 91% of the total number of scientists, engineers, and technicians, while 115 countries with over two-thirds of world population possess about 9% of these qualified personnel.

Sources: UNESCO *Statistical Yearbook* and Ruth L. Sivard, *World Military and Social Expenditures*, 1978.

teaching. World expenditures on public education were nearly $380 billion in 1978 – only the extraordinary sums spent for military purposes surpass this total.

What is striking from this global viewpoint is not so much the size of the schooling enterprise but its unparalleled mal-distribution between the developed and developing countries, and the situation is even more unbalanced in educational terms than in economic terms. The array of educational statistics, shown on page 64, is telling.

Neither calls for a New International Order nor demands for school reform can afford to neglect this unacceptable situation. It has become indispensable for each country to undertake initiatives in education to develop new global and innovative perspectives in learning as long term investments toward resolving global problems. At the same time, all the reform in all the world's existing schooling will in the long run only deepen global inequities if an important part of the world's population continues to be denied access to any kind of formal education.

Local rigidity: The schools' goal of preparation for life is turning to separation from life.

Let us switch from the global to the local view to examine a problem of very different but equally serious dimensions. As the local neighborhood school expands, becomes more expensive, consolidates, and absorbs more responsibilities cast off by new family demands, it tends to become increasingly institutionalized and rigid.* Long years of such developments in schools have led to whole institutional systems that are among the most conservative and rigid in society.

The consequence of such developments is that the schools' goal of preparation for life is turning to separation from life. This isolation is particularly pronounced in the lack of integration between the world of work and the world of school.† The schools systematically separate the young from the workplace, as does the workplace commonly reject the intrusion of pupils. In many societies, the barriers between school

---

* This situation is intensifying in some industrial countries where "zero growth" in school-age populations or in financial resources is compounding the problem.

† It is to be deplored that the exploitation of child labor still exists in a number of countries where working children are denied the chance to go to school.

and work are so strong that the only source of information available to the young about different careers and modes of work come from peers, television, or the example of parents. The fact that intellectual work is considered superior to manual labor is not surprising in societies in which school has come to monopolize the time of the young.

The preoccupation with the training of the young and the neglect of the needs of adults are problems widely recognized by many scholars of educational policy* who have developed and supported the concept known as lifelong learning. In a period of rapid changes and rising complexity, it no longer makes sense to cram education into the first eighteen to twenty-odd years of life. Nearly everyone who has studied the misdistribution of schooling over a lifetime agrees that the system should be reorganized and the years of education reallocated over the period of a normal lifespan. Yet the road to lifelong learning can best be described as rocky. With

"Lifelong learning", a conceptual approach likely to enhance innovation, has not yet penetrated many societies.

possible exceptions of such programs in Scandinavia and the resurgence of continuing education in North America, experimentation with educational structures has shown that the prevailing systems are generally still too rigid to accept lifelong learning as a viable, widely available option.

Yet, despite the rigidities that limit education to the exisiting forms of schooling, experiments with a variety of alternative educational programs continue and deserve further support. Community colleges, adult education, and alternative schools in many industrial countries represent a growing "learning laboratory" where innovative ideas are born and tested. At the same time, such experimentation that seems to grow naturally in the North may be presently unattainable due to the cost factor in Third World countries where conventional schooling saps all of their financial resources for education. One of the weakest links in the educational chain is the miniscule amounts of resources that have been made available for "research and development" in both education and learning.†

---

* See for example Torsten Husén, *The Learning Society,* Methuen & Co., 1974.
† See page 102.

*Conventional schooling is
still preoccupied with language:
whatever happened to values?*

The tendency for schools to become separated from life is reinforced by another type of rigidity — the schools' preoccupation with language to the neglect of the other elements of learning. As already discussed, the elements of the learning process extend well beyond the manipulation of linguistic and numerical symbols (verbal and mathematical skills).

The question of values is crucial for moving from maintenance to innovative learning. The current school is not value-neutral: it systematically, if implicitly, reinforces predominant, often out-dated, values. With the exception of some promising experiments, especially in North America, relatively few schools have been able to develop sustained programs whereby the young acquire practice in making ethical choices, especially if those choices call basic and fundamental values into question. At one extreme, value analyses may be so "taboo" in some societies that the young grow up without consciously identifying their own values and without realizing that others may hold conflicting values with equal conviction. Neither in school, nor in the family, have they been encouraged or challenged to clarify their values and the consequences they imply. It must be recorded in this context that the neglect of values is not necessarily the fault of the schools alone; in many societies, it is the parents who object to the inclusion of values in the curriculum.

Some Effects of Blocking Innovative Learning

*Two effects of blocking inno-
vative learning: irrelevance
and waste of human potential.*

The degree to which societies have neglected innovative learning in favor of maintenance learning can be seen by the extent of irrelevance in their educational systems and their waste of human learning potential. On a worldwide scale, the overemphasis on maintenance learning today has resulted in an extraordinary level of irrelevance and waste.

Irrelevance: Diversion of Current Priorities from Future Needs

Consider the case of a child born in 1980 who will be scarcely out of adolescence in the year 2000, a working adult until 2040, and a village elder or senior citizen until around mid-century.* By the time this child is an adolescent, it is a virtual certainty that more people will have been added to the world's population than were alive in 1914; that nuclear weapons will have proliferated to around 50 countries; that energy derived from petroleum and natural gas will have become scarce and very expensive; and that, with a world telecommunication network far more extensive than today, the opportunities for information exchange, as well as the threats to cultural identity, will have intensified. What, if anything, is being done in the formal education systems and other learning arrangements to prepare children to deal with these and similar issues?

Most education systems are not only unprepared to deal with global issues such as these, but are reluctant to accept responsibility for initiating programs that examine the future. One reason for this neglect of future issues in formal education is the implicit and unquestioned faith in learning by shock. Those in educational policy, administration, and teaching hesitate to switch from a successful history of looking to the past in order to solve problems, and are reluctant to look to the future, which has always seemed to take care of itself. Why initiate learning in the schools about nuclear war, for example, if you are among those who accept the proposition that only a nuclear holocaust will teach humanity to stop the arms race?

The implicit acceptance of this fatalistic viewpoint accounts in large measure for much of the irrelevance found in formal educational systems worldwide. They continue to maintain practices and methods that can best be described as obsolete, over-specialized, incomplete, or inappropriate — in short, irrelevant. Long "learning lags" are accepted as inevitable; interdisciplinary studies are rejected in favor of specialization; vital issues and perspectives are neglected or in some cases considered taboo; all these problems are compounded in parts of the Third World where carbon copy educational systems are doubly irrelevant.

Changes in educational systems come slowly. From the moment when
_____
* World life expectancy is roughly 60 years; thus, around half of those born in 1980 will still be alive by the middle of the 21st century.

the need for a change is first perceived, the time that elapses until the need is acknowledged and the change is implemented is known as a "learning lag". There are many cases where such learning lags may be thirty years or longer,* by which time the original reason for the change may have disappeared. For example, had basic issues related to nuclear energy been introduced into school curricula and through the mass media in the 1950s, a more informed public discussion could have taken place in the 1960s and 1970s *before* decisions to build nuclear power plants were taken and waste disposal problems created. Is it not time to introduce study at all levels about the theory and functioning of alternative energy sources such as solar energy, to improve the chances that discovery of any unexpected disadvantage will occur before new technologies are introduced and before new installations are in place?

Unnecessarily long "lags" associated with maintenance learning are pre-empting society's options to deal with global issues.

The length and severity of lags in learning, however, can vary significantly. They are neither fixed nor inevitable. There are many programs and policies that can speed up innovation in learning. For example, re-training teachers already in service, rather than waiting for the natural course of retirement and replacement, is one essential step to cut lags in learning. In those industrial countries facing zero growth in school age population, however, the trend is in precisely the opposite direction. As growth in schools slows, fewer younger new teachers are added, and those already in the system resist innovations that might threaten their job security. At a time when creative ideas are needed quickly, many administrators, teachers, and their unions are resisting change. One challenge for all those in formal education is how to implement such change during an era of employment insecurity.

Learning lags exist outside the schools as well. Parents bring beliefs, values, and outlooks from an earlier generation to their children. Parents in consumer-oriented societies, for example, are likely to pass on to their offspring the "throw-away", high consumption values that conflict increasingly with contemporary societal needs. And in both developing

---

* See examples given by Torsten Husén in *The Learning Society, op. cit.*

and industrial countries, conventional patterns of child-rearing may be projected beyond the family setting to the schools: parents will exert pressure on school administrators and teachers to resist change and stay within the bounds of tradition.

Television and other mass media, usually perceived as a source of the most up-to-date information, can also contribute to learning lags. In developing countries with rapidly expanding broadcasting facilities, the airways include a significant portion of 20–30-year-old imported films that project out-of-date stereotypes of consumption patterns, racial attitudes, and aggressive behavior. One mark of real competence among teachers, as well as parents and managers of the media, will increasingly be an ability not only to minimize obsolescent values and images, but more importantly to reverse learning lags to help anticipate and shape future values needed to narrow the human gap.

Inter-disciplinary perspectives are needed for innovative learning.

As the quantity of knowledge becomes greater and its organization more complex, the pressures to specialize increase. Knowledge becomes fragmented into disciplines, and the learning processes are confined even to sub-disciplines. The truth of the saying that we know more and more about less and less has reached serious proportions. While some societies have gingerly experimented with inter-disciplinary and trans-disciplinary studies, the modern trend toward fragmentation continues. Disciplinary boundaries are becoming more impenetrable, reinforced by the values and criteria of the academic world.

Nowhere is the impact of over-specialization so keenly felt as in the context of global issues. It is simply not possible to analyze and formulate policies for global issues from any exclusive disciplinary perspective. The economic approach, the legal approach, the social or political approach are each, by themselves, insufficient for dealing with problems that require an integrated and holistic understanding. Such specialization virtually guarantees irrelevance.

One of the greatest sources of irrelevance in education is not only that obsolete subjects remain but that they obstruct the incorporation of newer, more relevant concerns. Educators say, for instance, that school curricula are already overburdened. There often seems to be no space for the study of key global problems such as the arms race or the emancipation of women. It may be no exaggeration to assert that when the curriculum is already staggering with the weight of the past, there seems to be no room left for the needs of the future.

Referring to an over-emphasis upon the past in formal education should not be taken as an attack on the study of history. On the contrary, history can offer many examples where specific societies failed to prepare for and act decisively in unprecedented situations. Past civilizations present vivid lessons in what happens when human material needs are neglected, when social systems deny human dignity to all but a minority, and when preparations for war become the central concern of the state.

Some societies, notably those with a recent history of colonialism, are burdened with irrelevance of a double dimension: not only are their educational systems obsolete, but they are fundamentally inappropriate to the cultures into which they have been transplanted. The wholesale, carbon copy transfer of foreign learning models and the subsequent indiscriminate devaluation of traditional learning has left many developing countries with the ultimate in non-anticipatory and non-participatory learning.

Carbon copy systems of education in some Third World countries are obsolete and inappropriate.

The predominantly French and British schools that exist all across Africa and Asia are reminiscent of an earlier era. In the home countries, the educational systems underwent changes over the years; in the host countries, these systems were preserved intact to such an extent that many countries find themselves today with a retrospective school system whose perspective begins in the nineteenth century. The host countries chronically seem to lag at least one or two reforms behind the former colonial powers.

Nowhere is the severity of this discontinuity between schooling and everyday life more intense than in the problem of languages. While national or local mother tongues are spoken at home and in daily discourse, many schools abandon them in class, to the detriment of cultural identity and social integration, and contrary to sound pedagogy. The use and development of these languages all too often is, but should not be, viewed as competing with the major international languages which are essential for inter-cultural communications and the advancement of knowledge. Local and international languages ought rather to be seen as complementary. Overcoming old biases for one or the other path will require establishing clear objectives with considerable foresight because the efficient use of a plurality of languages demands fundamental, far-reaching decisions about the design of educational programs and the production of reading materials.

The presumed superiority of foreign schooling, examinations, and credentials for jobs — as well as the presumed superiority of information, media, and technical training from the post-colonial superpowers — has led to a devaluation of traditional and indigenous learning. The attitudes of many scholars in the developed, as well as some even in the developing, countries could until the most recent years be summed up in the deprecating statement of a British historian in the nineteenth century:

"... a single shelf of a good European library was worth the whole native literature of India and Arabia ... It is, I believe, no exaggeration to say, that all the historical information which has been collected from all the books written in the Sanskrit language is less valuable than what may be found in the most paltry abridgements used at preparatory schools in England ..."*

The need to restore learning relevant to national cultural needs — as well as to future needs of specific cultures undergoing especially rapid change — is leading many forward-looking Third World educators to re-examine traditional methods discarded without proper evaluation. The object of such an exercise is not to attempt to reinstate archaic practices which have outlived their purpose, but to identify some of the traditions that may still be relevant and culturally significant for self-reliant innovative learning.

Waste of Human Learning Potential:
The Example of Illiteracy and the Case of Women

A second effect of the blockages to innovative learning that often

---

* Thomas B. Macauley, "Minute on Indian Education", reprinted in *Prose and Poetry*, Harvard University Press, Cambridge, 1952.

parallels irrelevance is the waste of human learning potential. Most people think of waste in physical terms, such as waste of resources, energy, or money. Indeed, the global problematique has focused attention on the wasteful misuse of non-renewable physical resources such as oil, and on the wastes of industry that pollute the environment and threaten the capacity of the biosphere to absorb the by-products of exponential growth.

But another kind of waste has an even more serious impact on the whole knot of global problems and thus on the human gap – the waste of human learning potential. In this context, waste can result not only from the misuse that relegates people to marginal positions, but also from the lack of use or neglect of human capacities. At its worst, the neglect of the human mind perpetuates a cycle of ignorance and poverty: unacceptably large numbers of people find themselves excluded from all but the most rudimentary, informal opportunities to develop their learning processes. Not much better off are many other people whose participation in the systems of learning is seriously circumscribed and limited to levels far below their capacities or global needs. The dimensions of this critical waste of human learning potential can be illustrated by the changing dimensions of illiteracy and by an increasingly sensitive issue which we term "selective participation".

*Illiterates: "The Wasted Generation"**

Conventional illiteracy, both a symptom and a cause of the downward spiral of ignorance and poverty, epitomizes the waste of human learning potential. Despite world-wide attention devoted to curtailing illiteracy, it is a social affliction that is increasing year by year as population growth in the developing countries outstrips annual gains in literacy. UNESCO estimates that in 1980 there will be 820 million adult illiterates – a full one-fifth of the world's total population. Not only is the problem growing quantitatively, but the qualitative consequences of illiteracy become more serious as rural villagers (who constitute the bulk of the populations unable to read and write) are drawn more deeply

---

* Expression used by Philip H. Coombs in *The World Educational Crisis: A Systems Analysis,* Oxford University Press, 1968.

*Illiteracy is growing quantita-
tively and becoming more
serious qualitatively.*

into the global problematique:
They may be the first to suffer
the effects of world food
shortages, for example, yet
they have little influence over
decisions being made to up-grade rural food production. They are being
called upon to participate in economic and social development schemes
and to take part in family planning programs, and yet they have neither
the reading skills nor access to written material that have become the
staples of the modern decision-making process.

It is worth highlighting briefly one special problem of waste associated
with illiteracy in developing countries – the problem of school drop-outs.
In some African countries, for example, a majority of children drop out
of elementary school before finishing the fourth year. For every 100
pupils completing a four-year cycle, African educational authorities
must count on starting with between 1½ and 3 times this number of
pupils to account for those who will drop out or fall behind. Financially,
this translates into an escalation of costs by as much as 300% per
elementary school graduate, a financial waste that countries hard pressed
for resources can ill afford.

A second, less familiar, face of illiteracy is beginning to appear in
some developed countries. What is termed "functional illiteracy" –
the inability to read or write well enough to apply for a job – is on the
increase. The only data available to date come from the USA, where recent
investigations show that some 23 million adults (10% of the population)
are functionally illiterate.* Further, a staggering 13% of American
17-year-olds *in school* (up to 30% among Hispanic or Black students)
cannot read well enough to participate in the everyday work of society.
Schooled illiteracy is double waste: twelve years of time, effort, and
finances are lost. And the personal consequences are tragic. Functional
illiterates remain on the fringes of a society brought up on the printed
word. They live in fear that someday, someone will discover their
secret shame.

Among the many issues surrounding the problems of both illiteracy
and functional illiteracy, two are especially noteworthy in relation to

---

* Official estimates reported to and listed by UNESCO show illiteracy, as conventionally defined, at 1% in the USA.

the concept of the human gap. The first is the apparent reluctance of most decision-makers to commit themselves and their societies to a full-scale program to eradicate illiteracy. Despite the fact that literacy is seen to go hand in hand with economic development, the impetus to create especially the type of literacy that could spark social participation and change is lacking in all but a few cases. Many of those in power are afraid to face the changes, and the rise in expectations, which would result from expanded literacy. This lack of political will is an illustration of how the refusal to use available power can lead to waste in learning.

Many in power distrust the changes and rising expectations that widespread literacy would bring.

The second issue concerns the current conventional criteria for literacy. Is "literacy" to be understood purely and simply as the ability to read and write? Again the distinction between maintenance and innovative learning is marked. Whereas maintenance learning, with its stress on language, equates literacy with reading and writing, innovative learning encompasses a basic competence in all the elements of learning within the framework of literacy. In innovative learning, the stress is on the value or *ethical dimension of literacy,* not unlike those concepts of literacy that focus on raising consciousness* and increasing the capacity to participate effectively and productively in society. The illiteracy at issue here concerns those people in the developed and developing countries alike who are evidently incapable of comprehending simple ethics.

The current criteria for literacy should be reviewed and an ethical dimension added.

There are contradictions inherent in the maintenance definition of literacy. There are, for example, many people still living within oral traditions, "illiterates" who have memorized religious or ethical epics or texts and who can philosophize and act at high levels of morality. Any implication that this type of person can *a priori* be considered less able, less prepared, or less worthy than the one who can read and

* Most notable of these is Paulo Freire, *Pedagogy of the Oppressed,* Penguin Books, 1972; and *Education for Critical Consciousness,* Seabury Press, 1973, by the same author.

**The Familiar Features
of World Illiteracy**

● There were 700 million illiterates in 1965, 800 million in 1975, projected to 820 million in 1980. UNESCO projections by region for 1980 show illiteracy at 73% in Africa, 63% in South Asia, 23% in Latin America.

● Illiteracy reflects poverty: the poorest 20 countries are over 80% illiterate.

● In the Middle East, it is estimated that literacy efforts must increase by a factor of three to get ahead of population growth.

● UNESCO's Experimental World Literacy Program yielded invaluable knowledge but few quantitative results. Less than one-third of the prospective participants became literate. What became clear was that without pervasive political will to change, literacy programs are ineffective.

● The lack of reading material in villages must be overcome both by generating material locally and by bringing villages into the mainstream of information.

● Among the few literacy success stories of the last 100 years: Japan, Soviet Union, China, Cuba, Sri Lanka.

Sources: UNESCO *Statistical Yearbook, op. cit.*; *The Experimental World Literacy Program: A Critical Assessment*, UNESCO Press, UNDP, 1976; and L. Bataille, *A Turning Point for Literacy*, Pergamon Press, 1975.

yet display intolerance or racism is an anachronism whose time for change has come. There is a pressing need to instill a respect and tolerance for people of other creeds, members of other tribes or clans, and those of a different color, race, sex or religious belief. A minimum requirement for the ethical dimension in literacy would be to treat all fellow human beings with respect and without discrimination.

Waste from Selective Participation: The Case of Women

Another widespread feature characteristic of maintenance learning which wastes human learning potential is what we term "selective participation". Selective participation means favoring certain learners and hindering others. The clearest cases involve discrimination based on race, ethnicity, age, social background, or sex. The significance of selective participation can be illustrated by examining how maintenance learning practices have confined and limited the learning processes of women, resulting in waste with multiple consequences for the human gap.

Of every twenty girls born in the Third World to poor rural parents, only one goes to school.

For most of history, the learning of women has been centered on well-defined traditional sectors such as child-rearing, domestic duties, and peasant farming. Their access to conventional formal education, to experimental non-formal programs for adults, and to informal sources of information through the media and the workplace has either been denied or limited. Though recently expanding, only small numbers of women have been able to realize their full learning potential. While access to schools, for example, is widening, women are still represented less at the university level than in primary school. And even when women do receive training and jobs, these are likely to be confined to the fields of health, administration, or teaching, because these are the jobs for which current education prepares them.

The largest, most disadvantaged group on the contemporary scene of world education are girls born to poor parents in rural sections of developing countries. While precise data are lacking, we estimate that only 5 children of every 100 in this group will complete the fourth year of primary school, while the other 95 are likely to remain illiterate and confined to traditional women's roles.

Of the many numerous and complex consequences of limiting the learning of fully half of humanity, one of the most obvious is that women have been denied participation in the wider processes of decision-making in society. As significant as the general lack of participation is, however, we prefer to highlight here a more specific aspect, which is that women have also been unable to participate in defining and resolving the issues posed by the world problematique.

Large numbers of studies conducted mostly by men have pin-pointed the role that women play in the problematique. The World Bank has shown that expanding the educational opportunities of females correlates with lowered fertility — women who have completed primary school average about two children fewer than those who have not.* Studies in nutrition show that the mother's education can reduce significantly children's learning disabilities caused by malnutrition during the nine prenatal months and the year and a half after birth. Data from Latin America indicate that the educational achievement of boys and girls correlates with the educational level of the mother. Analyses of the Third World show the crucial role women play in economic development.† Work in North America calls attention to the role of the mother as the primary shopper for and consumer of the products of growth societies.

Despite the obviously critical role that females play in population, nutrition, education, development, and consumption, few women have been, or been encouraged to be, directly involved in dealing with these and other global issues. For example, very few women participate in the design and implementation of population programs. The definitions and policies for development are set by men who have little awareness that the type of development they seek may have the secondary consequences of marginalizing women. Some argue, not without reason, that allowing women to participate in the debate about the global problematique

---

* See Robert McNamara, "Address to the Massachusetts Institute of Technology" published by the World Bank, April 27, 1977.

† Ester Boserup, *Women's Role in Economic Development,* Allen & Unwin, London, 1970.

Some consequences of limiting the learning of women are the lack of participation not only in society but also in resolving the global problematique.

may bring in added dimension of anticipation. One possibility to be explored further is that a mother's investment of her life in years of child-bearing and child-rearing makes her more concerned about the long term future of those children, whereas men – who, as one American study has shown,* spend only 12 minutes a day on average in primary child care – can be led by their life experience to be less concerned about the future.

The participation of women in society and in these world debates is bound to increase as the global issue of the emancipation of women becomes better understood.† What is critical from a learning perspective is the extent to which the increasing participation of women may enhance the shift from maintenance to innovative learning rather than simply expanding the ranks of the maintenance learners.

Cross-currents of Thinking: Towards a New Learning Perspective

The foregoing assessment has concentrated on the predominance of conventional maintenance/shock learning and the obstacles that this approach represents. But even stable systems are not static and lacking in counter-movements. What about the contrary trends that seek to circumvent or remove obstacles? Where are the catalysts and catalyzers of innovative learning? What cross-currents in thinking are evident and how strong are they compared to the rising tide of maintenance learning?

Nearly every reader will be able to cite examples of innovative learning. In the course of the consultations for this report, many cases were brought to our attention. Some illustrated only parts of

---

* John Robinson, Janet Yerby, Margeret Feiweger, and Nancy Sommerick, *America's Use of Time*, Ann Arbor, Michigan: Institute for Social Research, University of Michigan, 1976.

† Elizabeth Dodson Gray, "Masculine/Feminine Dimensions of the World Problematique", mimeo to the U.S. Association for The Club of Rome, Washington D.C., 1979.

what we defined as innovative learning — the anticipatory capabilities of state and private multinational enterprise, for example, or the participatory nature of trade unions.

Looking at the three spheres of governments, intergovernmental agencies, and non-governmental organizations (the "NGOs"), it is the NGOs that appear to have the longer term, flexible, interdisciplinary perspectives and where both anticipation and participation are emerging. Not every NGO, of course, could be considered a source of innovative learning. Yet the number and importance of those which are innovative is growing with astonishing rapidity.* Many provide the forums where new ideas and creative alternatives can be explored and simulated without the constraints of the existing economic, social, cultural, military, or political obstacles.

Many "NGOs" (non-governmental organizations) offer good examples of experimental approaches to innovative learning.

The same innovative thinking can be seen in many relatively recent organizations,† especially those engaged in futures research. The progress of the cross-currents to maintenance learning can be measured in the encouragement, tolerance, and leeway afforded to such innovative thinking, while their denial is an indication of how strongly the obstacles to innovative learning are entrenched.

Public opinion at large also reflects these trends. As the demand for and access to participation rises, many people are supporting and joining this emerging constituency for global change. Basic to these trends, and to a peaceful process of global change, will be what we call a new learning perspective. The emphasis in this perspective must be on the enhancement of the innovative learning capacities of individuals and society, to minimize the risk of their having to learn by shock.

Towards Innovative Societal Learning

The conventional, often unarticulated, conception of how societies

---

*See the *Yearbook of International Organizations* published annually by the Union of International Organizations (Brussels).

† Many are barely "organizations", but work rather through loose affiliations or networks of people. Some make a point of calling themselves "non-organizations".

learn usually starts with one or more *centers of concentrated competence* as the emanaters of new discoveries, theories, beliefs, and solutions. These new ideas are then disseminated to larger circles of people and to the public at large. This model of societal learning distinguishes two separate steps: one of distinct discovery and another of less distinct dissemination. The roles people play in this process are likewise differentiated: some invent and others assimilate. The role of society at large is reduced to adjusting to and consuming the discoveries and knowledge produced in centers of expertise. It is easy to see that this conception entails more teaching than learning.

The unavoidable consequence of this view of societal learning is elitism, technocracy, and paternalism. What is omitted is the fact that meaning and values – decisive for learning – are products of society at large, not of specialized centers. Despite all their technical advantages, the bodies of knowledge, technologies, know-how, and theories produced by such centers contain inherent shortcomings – they are too often divorced from the social context. They tend to reproduce themselves according to their own internal logic. This autonomous and self-reproducing development accounts in large part for the fact that so much of societal learning is maintenance learning.

Innovative societal learning seeks to restore active learning to those in society conventionally confined to a passive role of assimilation. Key to this goal is participation that goes beyond mere invitations to accept given solutions or ingenious attempts to capture goodwill and support for given products. To encourage innovative societal learning, true participation must enable people to open and inspect the "black-boxes" of knowledge, to question their relevance and meaning, and to re-design, re-combine, and re-order them where necessary. Effective participation therefore does not mean paying lip service to those who in the past have been deemed to count less than others, but rather ensuring a real contribution of the entire society.

Some will claim that the prevailing approach already assesses the expectation and needs – the values and meaning – of the society at large much as industrial marketing is preceded by surveys and tests of consumer preferences. But centers of expertise tend toward great selectivity, pursuing those societal preferences which already accord with their own critical assumptions, bending where necessary the facts to fit their own model.

Global issues, seen as a challenge to innovative societal learning, have to be reconsidered and seen not solely in terms of analytical devices such as global models, theoretical constructs, and given problems to be solved. They must also be viewed from the vantage point of those who can endow them with meaning and value, integrating them into real-life local contexts. "Grass-root" views and opinions cannot be treated as mere feedback to correct the pertinence of global models, but must be considered as a creative and innovative starting point.

IV

Illustrations of a New Learning Perspective

Except in response to revolution or crisis, improvements in human learning processes, as well as changes in the many educational systems intended to enchance those processes, have occurred slowly and often unconsciously. Moreover, and perhaps more significantly, any such changes — whether they came from revolution or evolution — tended to be limited to a particular geographic region or more commonly to a single society. In discussing ways to implement or to encourage the development of innovative learning, one has to ask whether there is not some alternative that is faster and more far-reaching than evolution and that is less costly, safer, and more equitable than shock.

The foregoing discussions of global issues and learning indicate not only that human learning processes have been unable to keep pace with complexity and danger, but also that their failure to do so has augmented the political, economic, and socio-cultural tensions that characterize present societies. To put it another way, the intensification of global issues is caused not only by an accelerating pace of change but also by stagnation in the pace of learning.

What these statements imply, corroborated by the many views and extensive information assembled as part of this report, is that a change in kind is called for rather than a mere change in degree. That is, simple additions to lifelong learning experiences or small changes to existing curricula will not be sufficient to bridge the human gap. The only rational way to develop innovative learning is through a conscious transformation, which we take to mean the creation of a critical mass of people who have developed a new learning perspective. This perspective must be cultivated by a form of learning and education which begins with a global raison d'être, which balances local, national, international, and global requirements, and which fosters an integrative and complete development of human beings. The question is whether and how such a transformation can itself occur through an anticipatory and participatory process, thereby enabling us to transcend the confines of present structures and to discover and create new options.

The need for a positive learning perspective is universal because the issues which condition the future of humanity are global. Although one must inevitably differentiate among the many approaches to learning in our heterogeneous world, one can safely state that developing and developed countries alike are deficient in innovative learning. The countries most advanced economically are not correspondingly more advanced in the development and use of their learning potential. Indeed relative to their importance, the industrial countries may be further behind. That is, it is largely because of their incapacity to learn how to master the advancement and usage of knowledge in their own interest as well as that of humanity as a whole that creates many global problems such as ultimate weapons, dehumanizing technologies, destruction of world habitats, over-consumption of natural resources, and obstructions to restructuring the international order. Their reliance on maintenance learning enables them to run the world political and life-support systems, but at the cost of running them down.

Global issues require far-reaching and universal changes in learning. Developed and developing countries alike are deficient in innovative learning.

The case of the developing countries, although less destructive, is no more defensible. Third World countries are wasting huge quantities of their learning potential, and are rapidly and indiscriminately discarding a traditional culture and the learning capacity inherent in it without replacing them by authentic, self-generated, viable ways and means of learning.

The development of a new learning perspective is well within contemporary human capacity, the limits of which are presently unknown. It will require a new political will — the political will to *initiate change* — and it implies putting faith and trust in the capacity of human beings to implement changes consciously. Wherever the lack of political will to initiate change is linked with attempts to maintain power, the problem is particularly severe. When participation is minimized by political repression, or when anticipation is prevented by political cycles favoring short term views, then the transformation required for a new learning perspective will be correspondingly difficult. While an enhancement in learning ability on a global scale will be a monumental task, no other viable alternative, as currently foreseeable, offers greater hope for success.

It must be made clear that we are *not proposing an undifferentiated blueprint* for a world learning program. We must stress the fact that even if there is unity in the overall objectives of innovative learning, there will necessarily be a great diversity of specific programs and implementations. The new learning perspective must be both purposive and offer alternative choices.

The Context for Change

Learning that promotes the goals of survival and dignity cannot be developed and encouraged in a vacuum.* For example, it makes little sense to launch a major program to stimulate learning among people living below the subsistence level without at the same time adopting policies conducive to the eradication of poverty and to an improvement in their levels of food, health, and habitat. The reverse is also true: raising the levels of food, health, and habitat implies a greater level of learning for people to autonomously maintain these higher material levels. While the linkages between learning and material factors are most easily seen in the case of people with unmet basic human needs, there exist for all people similar intrinsic relations between their need to learn and their material as well as non-material wants. These connections constitute the basic conditions, or contexts, within which learning occurs. Without a favorable context, the development of a new learning perspective is hampered. Some of these conditions, and the actions necessary to create them at the present time, are as follows:

---

* The Mexican educator, Tablo Latapí, relates the concept of learning to the intrinsic complementarity among at least four aspects of human action which are indispensable for real human development: 1) material transformation; 2) transformation of social structures; 3) transformation in socio-psychological processes which accompany changes in social structures; and 4) changes in values and aspirations. (Personal correspondence to the Learning Project, July, 1977.)

**The Learning Context:
Conditions or Policies that Promote
A New Learning Perspective**

● Eradicating poverty and meeting the most basic human material needs (food, health, shelter, and employment) and non-material needs (literacy, universal schooling*, and human rights) in the shortest time possible.

● Making people more aware of the structural conditioning and manipulation of their behavior in order to reduce the elitism in the world of learning that results from social and political controls over the non-participatory selection of learning objectives.

● Helping individuals locate themselves (instead of being assigned a location) in relation to society, to time and space, and to what they need to know.

● Respecting cultural identity and diversity; and recognizing the requirements of globality.

● Devising new norms and participatory arrangements to facilitate the sharing of knowledge and know-how nationally and internationally. Such sharing necessarily implies some redefinition or dilution of power, as well as reconsideration of those classical attributions of sovereignty which have become obsolete.

---

*Not necessarily the current pattern of schooling; note objections to current conceptions of schooling discussed on pages 63-67.

Establishing policies and programs to enhance innovative learning, as well as creating the conditions just suggested, are dependent upon at least one premise: a willingness to initiate fundamental processes of change, even when all of their implications are not known with total certainty in advance. The path of innovative learning necessarily entails a certain "risk of innovation". Without some minimal risk, there can be no new learning perspective. As concerns and priorities begin to shift from material and economic motivations to non-material and cultural objectives, such risks become increasingly difficult to comprehend and assess; however, compared to learning by shock, the risks involved in innovative learning are surely minimal.

Another premise bears examination. It is undeniable that while learning processes follow a universal pattern, the ways and means of learning are usually specific to the cultural terrain and national situation.* Certainly most if not all contemporary formal educational systems are nationally based, even when not always controlled by the nation state. Yet arguing for innovative learning processes and a new learning perspective that can cope with a global problematique automatically creates the need to strike some balance between international solidarity and responsibilities on the one hand, and national rights and duties on the other. What constitute norms for humanity's advancement and learning and what is properly left to national authorities in conducting learning programs in harmony with their overall objectives?

If there are to be any interventions at all to stimulate innovative learning, there is little question that they will, for the foreseeable future, have to occur at the national level. Each society should be free to design its own educational systems as a cornerstone of cultural integrity. Nevertheless, it must be granted that the matters to be learned and the process itself of learning, like every sector in the contemporary world, are subject to ever-increasing global influences. These global dimensions of the need to learn include qualitative changes in ways of thinking and a willingness to cooperate that is necessary for survival and dignity.

---

* Or sub-national where applicable such as in federations like India, the Federal Republic of Germany, or the United States as well as in other cases where education is highly decentralized. Further references here to the national level should be assumed to cover the sub-national, regional, state, provincial, or local level where applicable.

Because the world is presently characterized by so many imbalances, inequities, and injustices, the *The global dimension is essential to innovative learning.* global dimension in learning must be given more priority, especially in view of global issues which by definition cannot be resolved nationally or unilaterally.

But the real significance of the global dimension of learning may be illustrated by highlighting the role of learning in the attainment of a "new international order". The calls for restructuring the international order, which started with political decolonization and are being followed by quests for new economic, cultural, and communication and information orders, have become the leitmotif of the contemporary international agenda. The demands for and resistances to the redistribution that such new orders imply are largely a function of the values, mental attitudes and socio-economic institutions established and reinforced through learning processes. Without a new learning perspective — one that would permit all nations and people to grasp how they should change those of their prevailing values no longer consistent with the changing realities and exigencies of the contemporary world — it is highly unlikely that any new international order can be peacefully and harmoniously established. Systems of values hold the answer as to whether the future relations among and within societies will be conflictory or consentient in nature.

In contrast to the stress that the calls for a new international order place on redistribution and on transfer of technologies and capital, it must be noted that learning can be neither redistributed nor transferred in the same sense. Learning cannot be transferred, for learning is by its nature a process intrinsic to and cultivated by individuals. Knowledge, as an end product of learning, could be said to be transferable. However, there is a growing opinion* that "transfer" of technology has come to imply *blind acceptance* of foreign techniques and products — that is, acceptance without sufficient understanding of how they work, how they can be adapted to local conditions, or how they should be maintained. Thus to the extent "transfer of knowledge" implies the acceptance of knowledge without understanding it, the term mis-represents what is so critically needed.

* See page 111 for references and further discussion on this issue.

The complex relationship between "transfer" and "understanding" was studied by Toynbee, who noted that when cultures are in contact, the "hard" elements (such as tools and technology) are the easiest to transfer while the "soft" components (such as values, spiritual beliefs, culture, and life styles) are the most resistant. Many products flow across national boundaries, but it is surprising how few ideas, accompanied by sufficient understanding, are able to flow internationally. Despite the fact that societies are becoming increasingly transparent to one another and that partial solutions to one nation's problems probably exist in another nation's experience, very few useful ideas in political and social spheres, for example, are being effectively transposed or even considered. In large part, it is the inadequacy of learning capacities which accounts for the low level of understanding not only of ideas and knowledge originating outside a particular culture but also of the values intrinsic to and embodied in technologies that are to often "transferred" inappropriately.

Insufficient learning capacity leads to technology and knowledge "transferred" without adequate understanding.

Since most national education systems are concerned with transmitting national values limited to maintenance learning, a new learning perspective will have to clearly identify and confront those values that constitute obstacles to further social change. Moreover, the value question is complicated by the fact that more and more countries are renewing efforts to protect their own integrity from the intrusion of external values, at the same time that the trend in other countries is growing for a re-examination of some of these very same values. For instance, societies with a recent colonial history may see global co-operation in learning as a potential threat until their cultural identity is more firmly established and until they perceive that any change in the mental attitudes of the industrialized countries reaches significant proportions.

This chapter will present some examples of programs and policies that could encourage anticipation and participation. It will also illustrate how innovative learning could be applied to help cope with global issues. It cannot be stressed strongly enough that these are not intended as blueprints for action but rather as illustrations, for each society will have to initiate action appropriate to its own situation.

**Illustrations of Programs to
Encourage a New Learning Perspective**

● Liberation of the Fifth World: Literacy

● School and Life

● University and Society

● The Mass Media and Visions of the Future

● Learning Research

Liberation of the "Fifth World": Literacy

The "Third World" is a term used to describe the developing countries as a whole. When the material wealth of some Third World countries could no longer be ignored, the term "Fourth World" came into being to designate the poorest countries with the fewest material resources. Given our emphasis on the human element in this report, it was a natural step to come to think of the "Fifth World" as a term encompassing the one-fifth of humanity poorest in certain non-material resources. Chief and basic among these is literacy defined in the conventional sense of the ability to read and write. One-fifth of the contemporary world's population lacks the fundamental right to communicate through the written word. This waste of human potential, described in the previous chapter, is as inexcusable as it is inestimable.

The means exist, and the political will is needed, to eradicate conventional illiteracy among the one-fifth of the world's population who cannot read or write.

The Fourth and Fifth Worlds tend to overlap in membership.* It is no mere coincidence that the illiterate populations are often the same ones that cannot satisfy their most basic needs for food, health, shelter, and employment. Nor is it simply coincidental that these populations tend to be composed primarily of rural people, and that the majority are women. The vicious circle of ignorance and poverty virtually ensures that the living conditions of those in the Fifth World will steadily deteriorate. What can be done to reverse this situation is different for the Fifth World than for the Fourth. In very broad terms, when the problem is poverty and lack of basic material resources, national and international redistribution can be crucial. But when the problem is illiteracy, the emphasis in the model shifts. Whereas redistribution of financial and technical resources to support literacy efforts can help, the critical element is the development of the inner capacities of the people themselves. Self-help is a key factor, for without it literacy and learning cannot be developed.

We would therefore concur with those who urge undertaking a world-wide literacy program which would stop the waste of human learning potential. It should place highest priority on the rural areas, and could be carried out within the framework of what is currently called "integrated rural development", which means that literacy should be linked to the fulfillment of other basic needs as well. It is neither proper nor necessary to assess such literacy programs in terms of immediate economic returns; while literacy may bring economic advantages in the long run, the most immediate concern is to start a process that leads to increasing human dignity and to breaking the vicious circle of poverty and marginalization.

But what about the wider concept of "literacy" that extends beyond reading and writing to include especially an ethical dimension among all the other elements of learning? It is altogether opportune and desirable for the international community to reconsider the basic criteria for literacy. Despite the difficulties inherent in articulating new measure-

---

* A quick, although controversial, measure of the distinctions between Fourth and Fifth Worlds can be obtained by using GNP per capita figures and literacy rates. Some countries are low in both and would fit both categories. Recently, several countries have achieved a high GNP but remained low in literacy, so could be thought of as Fifth but not Fourth World. And there are a few countries low in GNP but which have achieved high literacy rates: Fourth World but not Fifth.

able standards, efforts should be encouraged to conceive of literacy as a means of increasing people's consciousness and their ability to participate constructively and ethically.

This wider view of literacy implies that a "mapping" of what was termed the "Fifth World" ought to extend to the developed countries, encompassing many people

The criteria for literacy should be widened to include an ethical dimension, which would more accurately reflect why the human condition continues to deteriorate.

not conventionally considered illiterate. Focusing on this wider illiteracy — rather than limiting it to Third World people who although unable to read and write may have highly developed ethical standards — would more accurately reflect the more serious problems intrinsic to the deterioration of the human condition. Programs and policies need to be created in the industrial as well as developing countries to address the need for basic competence in participation and ethics. Particularly in developed countries, one vehicle for such programs might be the creation of learning centers, allied with adult and continuing education programs, where adults on a voluntary basis could assess the "state of health" of their learning, much in the way most people periodically have medical check-ups. Such centers could perform a "check-up" function that could be instrumental in enhancing a society's general learning capacity.

Contemporary history shows that conventional illiteracy has been wiped out only by generating the political will to encourage change. To achieve either type of literacy, the initiative to transform must be autonomous, coming from within the society. Programs for literacy in reading and writing and those stressing an ethical dimension should be conceived first and foremost as national self-reliant efforts, but with external support where appropriate. International cooperation and support are essential to complement self-reliance and self-help. Yet international action alone cannot achieve results in the absence of national willingness to act.

What if humanity were to continue to allow illiteracy to increase? What are the consequences of inaction? We would anticipate a steady and grave deterioration of the socio-cultural and ethical standards of humanity. With one-fifth of the world conventionally illiterate, and with many more lacking a basic awareness of ethics, no one can seriously speak of human solidarity. In the context of a new learning perspective, the fundamental purpose of literacy must go beyond "basic needs" and "human rights" — it is to provide a potent agent for the changes and preparation needed now and increasingly so in the future.

School and Life

The dichotomy between school and life stems primarily from the inability of schools to adapt to the reality of the world outside their walls. The previous chapter described some of the major obstacles that contribute to this separation such as the rigidities of schooling and the implicit constraints placed on values. Moreover, some countries face additional obstacles that separate school from life such as the foreign nature of many schools and the neglect of national and local mother tongues.

As a first step in re-orienting schools to overcome their separation from life, we would urge support for programs that integrate schooling and work more closely in order to combine theoretical training with the practice of living. For example, every child, at least by age 12, should spend on average one day per week during the school year at work outside the school. The nature of the work could vary considerably: it could be in industry, enterprises, service centers, research institutes, or in public or community service organizations. The purpose of such a program would be to ensure integration and relevance, by providing opportunities for participation in as many diverse contexts as possible. A further purpose would be to instill a sense of responsibility. The work is not to be viewed either in the economic sense as an attempt to increase productivity, or even, except for the older students, as training for a specific job. Clearly, strict precautions would have to be taken to avoid misuse of the program to exploit child labor, and to ensure, in cooperation with trade unions, that the program did not become a threat to employment of adults.

An operation of this nature and scope could not be run on a central-

On average, every child should be engaged one day per week outside the school.

ized basis. At least two levels of organization would be needed. The first would be to give primary responsibility to the directors of schools to make the arrangements with the local institutions and enterprises. A second level would be some regional coordinating body that would balance requests to place students. The work should be realistic and serious. Some minimal remuneration to the child or school would be desirable, but not essential, to promote responsibility. The child should experience the greatest variety of jobs and institutions as practicality permits, and the school's curriculum should reflect some of the work experiences. One effect of such a program would be to make the objectives of the schools more relevant to the learning needs of society.

A work-school program of this sort could also be used to foster anticipatory learning by using the work experience to strengthen an individual's capacity to detect and define real life problems and to propose and evaluate alternative future solutions. Problem detection, scenario building, and the systems thinking necessary to cope with future situations could be built into the curriculum. For instance, there exists in many countries a serious lag between developments in science and technology and their incorporation into the content and methods of schooling, and a case in point concerns computers and modeling. Wherever computers are available, why not let students use them as part of their classwork to project future trends in the organizations where they work? Even where computers are not readily available, the same principles of simulation and integrative systems thinking could be applied. Not only would such exercises stimulate anticipatory thinking, but they would also help overcome the "scientific illiteracy" that often results from the abstract way science is taught divorced from its applications in the working world.

University and Society

Universities, the pinnacle of the formal education systems, should be leading a campaign toward improving human capacities; instead, the world's forty million university students* and five thousand universi-

---

*Enrollment in university has grown rapidly from twelve million in 1960 to the current forty million. The rate of growth is higher in the developing countries, which will however still account for only one-quarter of the total. Growth rates in university enrollment have slowed somewhat in the 1970s to about 6% in the North and 9% in the South. In a few countries, they are declining.

ties are either held or holding back from playing a leading role for which they should be destined. Problems of selective participation, narrow specialization, chauvinism of academic disciplines, neglect of vital issues, "citadel mentality" of many administrators, and preoccupation with selfish social advancement all limit the relevance of one of humanity's major learning resources. The following proposals are intended to illustrate the role universities could play to help bridge the human gap by encouraging anticipation and participation.

Universities around the world, but especially Third World carbon copies of universities in industrial countries, are still too remote from the basic issues confronting their societies.* Many decision-makers see the university essentially as a factory for the production of future employees, even though adequate man-power plans or satisfactory job descriptions seldom exist. Universities are thus often remote from the *Universities need to be more directly involved in the developmental projects of society.* research and study activities concerned with political and socio-economic realities. We believe therefore that a major effort should be made to restore balance between action and reflection by involving both public and private universities more directly in the evolution of society through research contracts and development projects.

For example, who in the developing countries is better placed than the universities to implement literacy programs? Could not the students be given credits equivalent to two semester courses if they make ten persons literate by the end of the academic year? Could they not undertake field work connected with their studies for a number of weeks per year so as to extend the university out into the rural areas? The combination of just these two domestic innovations applied to the ten million university students of the Third World could, given adequate technical, financial, and administrative backstopping, reduce conventional illiteracy by half within five years and eradicate it within about ten.

---

* There are of course a few exceptions such as the experiment launched by Leopold Senghor in Senegal under the name of the "Université des Mutants" which has adopted an innovative learning approach based on the concept of "mutation" coupled with an emphasis on socio-cultural values.

Such programs need not of course be limited to literacy. They could apply to any of the areas of what might be called the "domestic problematique" such as water resources, land conservation, health and sanitation, environmental protection, preservation of the cultural heritage, and so on. Government agencies and private enterprises could contract with universities for work on any such developmental projects. While there are no statistics for the amount of studies and research projects contracted out by the developing countries to foreign consulting firms, the total surely has been significant. Some of those studies could have been undertaken in national universities able to provide the needed resources for research.*

The extent to which universities, properly strengthened and equipped, can and should participate in facing a domestic problematique and in fostering development raises the question of the role of the university. While we recognize the importance in advancing and transmitting knowledge, and in providing an atmosphere for free and unfettered reflection, we find that more stress should be placed on helping to understand, anticipate, and where possible resolve current problems in society.† The university should serve as a laboratory which analyzes the past, tests the present, and prepares alternative futures. To succeed in such a formidable task it has to be more closely involved — within its broad fields of competence — in the developmental process of society. This requires a minimum degree of autonomy, highly flexible rules, and rolling plans which can be regularly adjusted and re-oriented to focus on practical issues. No serious re-orientation of the work of universities can be envisaged until decisions, often political, are discussed and agreed upon about the nature and extent of a university's contribution to the economic and socio-cultural well-being of the population.

A university's capacity to help identify and assess global issues as

---

* Even in the United States, which has been a model example of the collaboration between universities and the public sector, there have been changes as can be seen from a recent statement by Jerome B. Wiesner, President of MIT (Massachusetts Institute of Technology), in which he declared that the government is "failing to use its university and college research to help in its economic development." *New York Times,* November 10, 1978.

† An encouraging example is the United Nations University which operates in the form of a network of institutions of higher education throughout the world and is concentrating its program on a number of key societal issues.

Universities and the "domestic problematique": the need to overcome the narrowness of academic disciplines.

they are manifested locally will be greatly enhanced when the chauvinism, nationalism, and sovereignty of academic disciplines yields to a transdisciplinary basis. Some reorganization of academic and administrative structures should be reconsidered to combine university departments according to issues rather than only and always according to disciplines. These newly constituted groupings could be considered as task forces, to be dissolved once their original objective is attained and to be recombined when new objectives are sought. Teaching as well as research work could then be organized around broad themes, thereby reducing the present segmentation and sectorialization of the curricula. Such a focus would bring the university closer to the basic concerns of society. It would also introduce some vital issues currently underemphasized on the university agenda — such as rural development, malnutrition, unemployment, illiteracy, housing and juvenile delinquency. These are but a few of the areas which require research and practical action and where the university population of students and teachers alike could be of great significance.

The Mass Media and Visions of the Future

There is little question that the mass media have a profound influence on how we view the future, which in turn will have a strong impact on its quality. Every society and individual has, implicitly or explicitly, a vision of at least desirable and probable futures (which, clearly, need not be the same). As the global telecommunications network expands to the point where it reaches nearly every person on the planet, it will become an increasingly powerful vehicle for influencing these visions of the future. The key questions

The mass media will increasingly influence our visions of the future.

are whether the mass media are prepared to work consciously toward an improvement in the quality of these visions, and whether people at large will be prepared to use rather than be used by the mass media.

Several new activities have emerged to help people think more explicitly, realistically, accurately and creatively about the future. These include the areas of future studies, computer modeling, scenario building, and systems analysis. These place a premium on holistic or integrative thinking. Some of the most important features of such thinking by which both individuals and especially societies will be judged are the following:

**Some Features
of Integrative Thinking**

● evaluation of the long term future consequences of present decisions;

● consideration of second-order consequences (what are called either side-effects or surprise effects);

● ability to make plans and strategies for the future, to monitor and modify plans (called "rolling planning"), and to conduct evaluations to detect early warning signs of possible problems;

● skill in "systemic" thinking, which is the capacity to see the whole as well as its parts, and to see multiple rather than single causes and effects;

● capacity to detect interrelationships and to assess their importance, which is often greater than that of the elements they interlink.

It is precisely in the application of integrative thinking to visions of the future where the mass media could offer their greatest contribution. We would urge that at both the national and international levels ways be found to encourage the conscious constructive use of the media in this direction. One way, for example, is to create roles for "ombudsmen" with experience in the media, future-oriented studies, and educational and human sciences. Such a function should be an autonomous one with an emphasis on flexible criteria. These might include guidelines for example that establish a redistribution of television programming such that roughly one-third is devoted to education, one-third to public and cultural affairs, and one-third to entertainment, depending of course on the cultural and social context.

Television and radio are already performing a learning function, whether intentional or not. Television and radio producers are *de facto* "educators". Given that their influence is so vast, it is essential that they use the potential they have to promote constructive rather than destructive visions of the future.

For example, the content of the mass media could give more attention to the issues of importance to the future, including global issues. Perhaps even more importantly, special television or radio programs should be developed for children which can be used both in and out of school classrooms. The programs could be narrated by some of the media characters already familiar to children. Videotapes produced in small modules might provide one of the mainstays in such an undertaking to develop the capacity to deal with the future.

In many cases, there needs to be a review of the structure and organization of the enterprises which control the hardware of the media and which produce the software or programs. Where necessary, some codes of conduct might be developed to improve the integrity of learning and educational components of media programming. Particularly in developing countries, strong attention needs to be given to selecting higher quality, more appropriate programs for local broadcasting, and to correcting the great imbalances which currently exist in the import and export of television programming.

Improvements in the mass media must be accompanied by people willing and prepared to use them constructively. The pace of technological change in the field of telecommunications is so rapid that many people are incapable of keeping up with its developments. Computers are a good case in point. Still only a handful of experts demonstrate an ability to use the immense power that computers can offer to promote anticipatory learning. Every effort should be undertaken – in schools, in adult education, and in the training programs of private enterprises and governmental agencies – to prepare for the extraordinary speed, power and accuracy of a "man-machine dialogue" which will increasingly link individuals to centers and libraries with data banks, videotapes, book images, and so on. In this regard, it will be desirable for the tele-communications systems to be kept as simple as possible for ordinary people to use them, to choose among them, and to develop their own alternative programs without the need for long training and special expertise.

Learning Research

A quick glimpse into all the sciences concerned with learning – but especially into the humanities and social sciences – reveals that the subject of learning is at present being researched on a scale far below that warranted by its importance and pervasiveness. This mismatch between challenge and effort is recognized and deplored by many observers. It is difficult to imagine a greater breakthrough for the humanities and social sciences than to make progress in acquiring an understanding of how learning processes work. There is no more significant task with vast consequences for social life that could be put on their agenda. Many researchers waver before the enormity of this task. A high degree of specialization in the research, and sharp divisions within and among disciplines, make the study of what is necessarily an interdisciplinary enterprise even more difficult.

A challenge for the year 2000 — to understand how learning processes work.

Especially within the humanities and social sciences, what has most characterized the different schools of thought is the plethora of forms of learning they propose. Despite the fact that many researchers are looking for some unity in the mechanisms underlying learning, no coherent explanation emerges from the research. The same plurality is reflected when learning is viewed in terms of an end state or achievement such as the acquisition of knowledge, attitudes, or skills. We are constantly faced with a bewildering variety of seemingly conflicting possibilities and aims. Moreover, each discipline uses different concepts and criteria for what is and is not said to be true. The only feature common to this wide array of learning theories is *newness* in the sense that all types of learning pursue the acquisition of something that was not existing, grasped, or apparent before.

This is not to doubt or dispute the valid contributions made, for example, by the behaviorist school, with its experimental success in conditioning animals, with the new methods of instruction such as programmed learning, with the stress put on positive rather than aversive reinforcement, and with the use of methods borrowed from the natural sciences. At the same time, other schools of thought in the social sciences and humanities are backing away from adopting the methods of natural science to conduct their research. They are emphasizing instead the social components of an individual's learning such as interaction, motivation, interests, and group influence. Whereas traditional theories portrayed learning as a process of performing responses and experiencing their effects, the social approach stresses the capacity to learn by observation, i.e., to acquire integrated patterns of behavior without having to form them gradually by tedious trial and error.

This immense work centered on learning deserves and needs new international support for and cooperation among scientists and educators. We urge the launching of an international learning research project, perhaps similar to the ones which UNESCO has undertaken for the biosphere (MAB), or for scientific and technological information (UNISIST). Why not launch such an initiative in several parts of the world at once, de-coupled from the constraints imposed by excessive bureaucracy, but carried out with close collaboration with the United Nations system, especially UNESCO and all other international governmental and nongovernmental organizations concerned with learning,such as for example the World Health Organization. The basic aim of such a project would be to discover how to improve our learning to enable humanity to reduce its inner gaps.

The two cornerstones of this undertaking could be neurophysiological brain research and socio-psychological research – with both according due weight to cultural and educational implications of learning. That is, emphasis should be on an interdisciplinary approach that seeks to integrate natural, social, and human sciences across conventional academic and institutional barriers. The first task of such a project might well be simply to collect, with the help of an organization like the International Bureau of Education, the relevant information about on-going research in this area. After an assessment of this information, some form of international council could suggest priority areas of research and the ways and means for their coordination and financing at the international level.

All the countries of the world, regardless of their level of economic development, ought to initiate national research programs to participate in this world-wide endeavor. Public expenditures on education alone was nearly 400 billion dollars in 1978 — on the average 5.7% of the world's gross national product.*

If one were to add to public expenditures the costs for all of the informal and private activities which enter into learning, the sum would likely exceed 600 billion dollars annually. It is not possible to calculate what portion of this figure is devoted presently to research and development for learning, because despite improvements in UNESCO's *Statistical Yearbook,* many countries do not furnish statistics for such expenditures. Yet if each country devoted between one-half and one percent of its public expenditures on education to learning research, the funds mobilized would represent a critical mass which could lead to meaningful results. Such a step would also enhance the role and importance of learning for economic, social, and cultural development. It would be a sign that humanity is beginning to take seriously not only one of its most important resources, but its destiny as well.

Adequate research and experimentation ought to be extended to investigating the learning processes of and within institutions. Each major organization should have a "built-in" learning unit to monitor its learning. This function is distinct from training and evaluation although all three need to be harmonized.

An international learning research project would be participatory to the extent it would call upon researchers from a great variety of disciplines from the entire world community to work together and to share their knowledge and the results of their findings. And it should be anticipatory because learning is *the* sector which is likely to have a decisive impact on our future. Combining work in neurophysiology, cybernetics, communications technology, and psychology — to mention but a few research areas that should be included — is an explosive mix that promises significant results if the proper support can be assembled.

* Six percent in the developed and 4% in the developing countries.

Learning to Cope with Global Issues: Three Examples

How could the concepts of innovative learning be applied to global issues? It is obviously not possible in this short report to examine, in terms of learning, the entire knot of issues that comprise the world problematique. We have chosen three examples. The first concerns the problem of energy, an issue generally seen primarily from economic, political, or ecological perspectives; here the generating of new energy options are examined as a societal learning process. In the second example, we look at the mal-distribution and mis-orientation of science and technology to see how increased attention to values and participation might increase the chances of improving the uses to which science and technology are put. In the third example, learning plays the greatest role. Problems of cultural identity are examined, and one conclusion is that while their resolution depends on many factors, learning is one of the most important among them.

Generating New Energy Options

The present search for new energy options — new sources of supply and new patterns of demand — can be understood as the culmination of a long process of societal learning. Over immense spans of time, societies have slowly learned how to harness the mechanical energy embodied in human and animal power, and to make use of the heat and light generated by fire from a variety of fuels. Whether the changes in the sources and uses of energy seemed imperceptibly slow (as they were before the 19th century) or whether they could be experienced in a single lifetime, these changes entailed a process of learning that displayed an adaptive character. It was the biological model of learning: evolution and adaptation, with humanity submitting (if ever less willingly) to the natural regime of wind and water flows. Just as organisms adapted to a favorable niche in the environment, so did industries settle near favorable supplies of energy — clearly visible, for example, in the early French textile industries that grew up lengthwise along the rivers.

But societies engulfed by the Industrial Revolution were not satisfied by restructuring their "energy learning" to a process of adapting to an environment given by Nature. No "learning society" can be satisfied by fixed solutions that do not easily permit modifications and improvements; or, as Karl Deutsch puts it, societal learning capacity calls for uncommitted resources available for re-combination in new forms.* By the 18th and 19th centuries, the newly industrializing countries put such uncommitted resources to use in searching for forms of energy not tied to any geographic source, energy that was available, transportable, easily distributable, and consumable. Coal and steam provided the answer. Steamboats were developed to travel independent of the wind, and industrial plants could be located near raw materials instead of near energy supplies. By the last half of the last century in the industrial countries, and more recently in this century for the developing countries, a successful conclusion to centuries of "energy learning" seemed near: huge networks of electricity or gas could be made available to nearly any consumer anywhere. This network was created in parallel with developments in the fields of transportation, communication, trade, education, and so on — and to a large degree, it stimulated and shaped these developments.

Now that nearly the entire world has adopted, and adapted to, an extensive system of secondary energy (electricity fired predominantly by petroleum) plus some heating and transportation systems driven by petroleum as a primary energy source, we face a new challenge. All societies are compelled to re-stimulate their learning about new energy options, for the events of the early 1970s shocked many societies out of their lethargy. The vulnerability of energy systems dependent on oil was exposed and those societies which could not decrease this dependency are beginning to react to the disruptions caused by shortages, higher prices, and impending scarcity. How should this situation be interpreted from a learning perspective? Will the same processes that brought us successively from wind and water to coal and steam and then to oil and oil-fired electricity be sufficient in

The past development of energy systems represents a clear case of adaptive learning which for most uses was largely an unconscious process.

* Karl W. Deutsch, *The Nerves of Government: Models of Political Communication and Control,* The Free Press, New York, 1966.

today's context? Should we rely on maintenance learning to generate alternative energy options? If this fails, what will be the price of learning by shock? What alternative does innovative learning offer, and what are its chances of success and its risks of failure? To attempt an answer to these questions, let us portray today's energy situation in terms of some of the learning concepts elaborated in this report.

Unlike the earlier historical period where the problem was how to free energy from geographical constraints, the current energy situation cannot be reduced to a single problem. One cannot say, for example, that the issue is solely or even primarily how to create greater quantities of cheap energy. There is, concomitantly, an entire knot of issues that includes, for example, security and weapons, pollution and ecology, food production and agriculture, political issues of centralization and decentralization, and the entire realm of consumer oriented, energy intensive life-styles. This globality in terms of inter-connections between energy and other issues is also global in the geographic sense – there are obvious interdependencies among people worldwide as well as inter-connections among the problems. While other sources of complexity could be cited (especially the ambiguity and uncertainty of supply), what we want to stress here is that no single, definite, clear-cut answer or policy is sufficient or possible to cope with the complexity of energy.

In the energy situation, the human gap manifests itself in terms of *timing*. It is the distance between the rapidity of events (such as the 1974 oil crisis) and the human ability to learn how to act quickly enough to shape the events. We are heirs to a recent history of short-sighted learning about energy. Structures that require enormous consumptions of primary energy (mainly oil and gas, less so coal) have been adopted without hesitation because of an unquestioning faith in the continuation of inexpensive supplies of petroleum and an unwarranted belief in the magnitude of the contribution of nuclear energy. The question now is whether the time required to change these rigid structures is greater than the time required to learn how to harness alternative forms of energy that meet all the complexity constraints.

The higher prices and impending scarcities of energy are the first fines imposed by shock learning.

We are paying today the fines for the initial phase of learning by shock. Prior to the OPEC oil price rise and embargo, the maintenance learning systems produced few studies or scenarios on the consequences of oil scarcity; and in the few cases they did, they were not taken seriously. Anticipation played little or no role. Another characteristic of shock learning revealed itself. In the absence of counter-measures, it tends to have a regressive effect in that it impacts the poor more severely than the wealthy.

At present, the trend is for society to persist predominantly with maintenance learning, a necessary activity under the circumstances, but insufficient to generate viable long-run energy options. We should not discuss lightly the immediate potential of one partial form of maintenance, namely energy conservation. Here the goal is to adjust the existing systems by reducing the fraction of total energy consumption required for each unit of activity or of GNP growth.* A clear example where we remain in the framework of maintenance learning is in the proposals for nuclear energy. The proposals are to use the same (or improved) type of centralized electricity generating plants driven by nuclear fuel. In this case, the problems to be solved by maintenance learning are seen as mainly problems of safety and security of operations, of disposal of nuclear waste, and of the final choice between plutonium or uranium fuel cycles (breeder reactors vs. conventional reactors) and eventually nuclear fusion.†

Maintenance learning has not ignored solar energy either. Many solar proposals still resist fundamentally new ideas. For example, the logic of the old technologies is still visible in the central-tower designs for huge solar-powered steam-electric generators. If these were built on a wide scale, they would demand large areas of solar collector space and massive quantities of aluminium and glass.‡ Thus a new solar option can be treated with old formulas that continue the disadvantages of huge, costly, centralized, material-consuming systems. But it is easy to see the reasons for the inertia that brings learning by shock: the alternative

---

* Today, on average, a 1% growth in GNP requires 1% growth in energy consumption. In France, the energy component has been reduced to 0.8%. Planners hope to reduce it to 0.5% as a world average by the year 2020.

† The nuclear accident in Harrisburg in April, 1979 is a clear indication of the dangers inherent in the breakdown of an excessive "maintenance syndrome".

‡ Such a 10 MW "solar-central" designed for a Californian town of 10,000 inhabitants would require 2300 collectors on some 70 acres of land.

options may call into question the very existence of entire systems such as, for example, automotive transportation.

What alternative ways to generate new energy options are suggested by innovative learning? The fact that the energy debate has emerged from expert circles and has entered the public forum as a global issue is a positive first sign. Innovative societal learning entails the engagement of public (and in this case, world) opinion, the injection of competing values into the debates, the preparation of the ground for major decisions (even for those implying fundamental transformation), and of course an increase in the number of experiments and ideas for new energy options. But it would be erroneous to think that participation in public

Innovation in energy calls for decentralization of learning and extensive participation.

debate is sufficient. The debates must carry to other centers of decision, such as the energy R & D sectors. Their re-orientation away from their pre-determined paths and towards unconventional energy options should proceed without delay. For example, new horizons that require expertise are already visible in creative R & D laboratories, such as in enzyme research, where feasibility of using the catalytic agents of low energy life processes can be studied for its wider application.* Likewise, the public debates reveal the inadequacy not only of the existing technologies but of the current analytic tools and methodologies as well. New branches, symbolized by the work in "energy analysis", need to be furthered.

It is unclear how capable any particular society will be in balancing its sometimes complementary, sometimes conflicting processes of anticipation and participation. We fully recognize that these alone cannot resolve the current energy predicament. But neither do the old patterns lead to viable solutions. What is the use of some central authority adopting a solution if the public refuses to assimilate it? Innovative learning presupposes that solutions are judged prior to their adoption, and that they are given values and meaning in the larger social and personal context.

For example, the current energy debate cannot ignore the multitude of different socio-political contexts. For individuals, the energy

* See Carl-Göran Heden, "Enzyme Engineering and the Anatomy of Equilibrium Technology", *Quarterly Review of Biophysics* (10, 2), 1977.

debate cannot be isolated from their outlooks on nature, their sensibilities toward environmental pollution, to their view on the desirability of centralized vs. decentralized forms of administration and production, or from their styles of life, transportation, habitat, and work. At the larger social level, it is not strictly the scarcity of energy which drives the learning process, but rather the meaning we attribute to scarcity in the context of other global issues (such as environment, food, natural resources, urbanization, and science and technology). Thus the approaches must by definition be interdisciplinary. The question is no longer the technical one of how to provide more energy or even to live with less: it is how to prepare for new energies of the renewable type, chosen to fit in harmony with the preferable — probably to be modified — ways of life.

Reorienting the Applications of Science and Technology

One of the most recent global issues is one of the most ironic. Science and technology, two hand-in-hand endeavors among whose original purposes was the reduction of complexity, now count among the causes for its increase. What has always been seen as an endless source of potential solutions is now seen by many as part of the problem. We are now confronted by a dysfunction between advances in science and technology and our inability to learn either how to control or cope with their consequences. Let us look briefly at what, more specifically, is the problem, and how it relates to learning.

The global issue of science and technology can be summarized in two words: mal-distribution and mis-orientation. Probably the single greatest mal-distribution in the world today — both within but especially among countries — is in the area of science and technology. The industrial countries of the North account for 95% of world expenditures on science and technology compared to only 5% in the South.*

Science and technology are mal-distributed and mis-oriented.

---

* It is not only a question of financial resources. The human resources are even more insufficient. A country like India has only 20 scientists and engineers per 10,000 inhabitants. Nigeria, the largest African country, has only 10. In contrast, UNESCO lists the Ukrainian S.S.R. at 392 per 10,000 inhabitants, followed by the Soviet Union and Japan with 372 each. (UNESCO *Statistical Yearbook*, 1979.)

These imbalances are reflected in research and development activities. Most developing countries cannot or do not yet grant sufficient priority to scientific and technological research. They spend an average of two dollars per capita on R & D, whereas developed countries spend over fifty times that average.* Moreover, through its lack of coherent "transfer policies", the Third World is indirectly financing a sizeable portion of this R & D effort in the North by supplying an increasing amount of qualified manpower. Jan Tinbergen in the RIO Report† estimates that the "brain drain" costs the developing countries $4.6 billion per year.

This picture of imbalance has other aspects to it. Both science and technology can be "nationalistic", split as they are by the same international divisions that reflect national prestige and power, and especially science is further split by individual academic disciplines.‡ These divisions add a dimension of non-communication to a situation already characterized by selective participation. In learning, "sharing is gaining". Science and technology as learning processes start with the compilation and rapid communication of information. There are at present some 35,000 scientific and technical journals and periodicals which publish about 2,000,000 articles each year, written by around 750,000 authors in over 50 languages. In terms of learning, however, this information is incomplete and deficient because it is essentially of an *intra*-disciplinary nature with very little emphasis on *inter*-disciplinary materials.

Transdisciplinary information can help to establish a true dialogue between science and the public at large according to the requirements

---

* For detailed information on R & D expenditures by country and by area of research see the UNESCO *Statistical Yearbook* (1978), pp. 657–695. The yearbook does not give a global figure for all the developing countries. From various extrapolations we estimate the total R & D expenditure of the Third World to be around 950 million dollars — about 0.3% of the total GNP; the corresponding figure for developed countries is 2%. Some examples are: USSR (4.6%); Hungary (3.4%); USA (2.4%); Poland (2.3%); Fed. Rep. of Germany (2.2%); Sweden (2.1%); Japan and UK (2%); and France (1.8%).

† Jan Tinbergen, *Restructuring the International Order*, a report to The Club of Rome, E.P. Dutton, 1976. See also the study submitted by the Secretariat of UNCTAD to the UNCTAD V Conference (Manila, May 1979) on "the reverse transfer of technology — the 'brain drain' ".

‡ The structure of scientific institutions is contrary to a new learning perspective in that it creates a rigid stereotypic blueprint of faculties, departments, academies, and research centers built around disciplines and not around problems. It is another case of the selective participation described in Chapter III.

of participatory learning. Scientific and technological information is one of the most efficient means to avoid a cleavage between "producers" and "users". The extreme case of polarization is conflict. Society cannot be divided between those familiar with science and those who do not understand it, without the risk of a grim confrontation. When military matters or proprietary rights are involved, communication is reduced to a bare minimum. Secrecy and the withholding of information are two obstacles that greatly impair science and technology as instruments of societal learning. This lack of communication is most pronounced in North-South relations where the political and economic tensions with science and technology components are causing the North-South dialogue to falter. In contrast, scientists have greatly contributed to the detente between East and West, especially through the Pugwash Movement. The scientific exchanges between the Soviet Union and the United States, for example, are today much more open and intense than a decade ago, although still far from being sufficient.

Important as these problems of mal-distribution are, the more significant issue is the basic mis-orientation of the application of science and technology. Where the relevant sectors of pure and applied sciences are needed most — in health, food, shelter, and education — they are least available. And where science is most available, it is employed for destructive ends (defense and arms).*

Where science is needed the most, it is least available; and where it is most available is in the arms race.

There is at present a gigantic distortion of science and technology brought up by their militarization. The arms race has become a scientific and technological competition, breaking the classical rules of the field by introducing secrecy and suspicion where cooperation and sharing would be the normal conduct. Military R & D with its huge and wasteful systems, seeking performances alien to peaceful applications, is distorting scientific thinking. Precious resources are wasted by a frantic arms race while basic problems in food, transportation, weather, health, and education are postponed.

---

* It is also employed for needs such as space research which are less pressing than for social research. For the role of science in defense and arms, see the figures on the number of science personnel and the amount of R & D in the military, p. 53.

This mis-orientation applies not only to the questionable choice of problems towards which science is directed; in addition, many countries particularly in the Third World are importing technologies that take no account of the impact on their systems of values, of the difficulties in mastering and controlling the consequences of such technologies, and of the paucity of indigenous research capacity. If science – which implies a particular vision of the world – is to contribute to the solution of contemporary world problems,* then both its national base as well as its international framework will have to be greatly enlarged.

One of the main problems of science and technology comes from their public image as an end product instead of a process of learning. Science itself is first and foremost the process of making *and unmaking* hypotheses, axioms, images, laws, and paradigms rather than products – it is a learning process. If this process is to be used to help meet global issues, it must be directed. On the contrary, the norm that has guided scientific developments to date has not been what "should be" but rather what "could be" done – not what is "desirable" but what is "possible".

Those who think that science, or even technology, can be transferred or bought are only seeing its end products, the impact over which they have no control. Science is in essence an endogenous process, by definition not transferable.† Its role, orientation, and distribution result from our learning capacities, our value systems, and our culture. If our learning were self-reliant and operating effectively, many of the problems associated with science and technology would disappear.

Looking more specifically at formal education, it is apparent that scientific illiteracy is widespread. Few educational systems have been successful either in instilling a sense of global ethics among those who

---

* This theme has been analyzed in the International Symposium *Science and Global Issues* (Tallin, USSR, 1979).

† The Report of the *Symposium on the Future Development Prospects of Africa Towards the Year 2000* organized jointly by the U.N. Regional Economic Commissions for Africa (ECA) and the Organization for African Unity (OAU) (Monrovia, Liberia, February 1979) states:
"The objective for the year 2000 is to rid the continent of the general approach that currently prevails and which accepts without question the concept and practice of 'transfer of technology' – an expression which the Symposium suggests should be struck out from the international vocabulary." (Document E/CN.14/698 Add.2, p. 6.)

go into science or in making the processes of science accessible to a broad base of learners. Science is still for the elite. In most countries it is seen as something highly specialized, difficult to comprehend, a "domaine réservé" whose entrance is marked by a "no trespassing" sign. Science and technology will remain a global problem until a far broader base of people come to understand their purpose and nature.

But it is not possible to wait for such long term developments. A few priorities should be chosen now to help re-orient science and technology. First among these priorities, for food deficit countries, could be a program of "science for food" that would concentrate on fostering autonomy and self-sufficiency in food production, equity in food distribution, and minimum use of energy in its production as well as care and conservation in its storage and processing. Such autonomy could literally save the lives of the estimated 12 million children who needlessly perish annually from starvation; and it could safeguard the learning capacity of the many more millions of victims of malnutrition. A side effect of no small importance would be to reduce the chances of potential conflict by negating the option of withholding food exports as part of power politics.

Other priorities for science might be established such as science for basic needs, where experimental "science learning units" could be established at the local or community level to help improve sanitation, housing, potable water, education, and employment. There is a very fundamental re-orientation in perspective that such programs would entail which might be called the re-orientation of science for human dignity. Particularly (but certainly not only) those who devoted their early science careers to the building of the atomic bomb and who now are devoting their considerable efforts to development, human rights, and peaceful programs will understand the meaning and significance of this perspective. In science, the social and ethical intertwine. This is why one can say that the future of science is also the future of ethics. When science is used to promote human dignity, the old dichotomy between science and culture will disappear.

In contrast with the organized effort of science for military purposes, very little has been done to use science and technology as a main lever of development, to apply them toward decreasing the existing gaps, and to propose new solutions for global issues. The role of science and technology at the global level will continue over at least the next decade to be an issue for international debate, marked by the 1979 UNCSTD* conference, one in the series of UN world conferences dedicated to science and technology for development. The objectives of UNCSTD are to produce a new climate favorable to the creation of an endogenous basis for research in the developing countries; to apply this research to their development; to remove obstacles hindering their access to technology; to promote the institutional changes required at national and international levels; and to examine the relations between science and technology and the future. Realization of these objectives will have a significant impact on the concepts of learning in general and on innovative learning in particular.

Science, like learning, is everyone's concern. The notion of restricting science to "science for science's sake" is just as meaningless as restricting the policy decisions which govern it to governmental circles when social justice and the survival of humanity are in question. The scientific community has a key learning role to play.†

To conceive science and technology as a simple industry of knowledge, to believe that it is enough to invest the funds to find the equipment and to hire the qualified manpower in order to achieve the desired outcomes is only a part of the logic of scientific discovery and progress. There is another side, not ready for measurement, in which change, intuition, association, trade of ideas, and the influence of the context, all concur to engender quantum jumps in thinking.

Respecting Cultural Identity

Cultural identity, a problem whose resolution will depend first and foremost on learning, has become a global issue with a double risk. On the one hand there is the threat of cultural homogenization, i.e., that the world might acquire a single uniform culture; and on the other, there is a more imminent danger of cultural and psychological disintegration

---

* United Nations Conference for the Application of Science and Technology for Development.
† See *Science, Technology and Global Problems: Issues of Development: Towards a New Role for Science and Technology*, ed. M. Goldsmith and A. King, Pergamon Press, 1979.

Cultural identity is a global issue with a double risk: global homogenization and local disintegration.

for both individuals as well as societies. These two are, of course, not unrelated.

This double risk can be expressed in stronger and more provocative terms. There is a form of behavior, often unconscious, which appears to others as cultural aggression. Another name for it could be mis-guided ethnocentrism. This behavior, mainly characteristic of the North, is a threat to international understanding and needs to be unlearned. At the same time, nearly all developing countries — and even some of the smaller developed ones — are suffering from cultural schizophrenia. They have indiscriminately discarded or abandoned some valuable cultural traditions. In their stead, they rely on foreign learning and cultural models that are alien to their way of life and thus a major source of incoherence and disorientation.

A world system vulnerable to the cultural aggression of some and the cultural disintegration of others is hardly a reliable basis for mutual understanding, dialogue, cooperation, joint ventures, or solidarity. It is obvious that this situation has some roots in colonialism. The Draft Cultural Charter for Africa* (1976) recalls that under colonial domination, all the African countries were faced with a political, economic, social, and cultural situation that led to the depersonalization of some parts of African society, to the falsification of its history, to the wasting of its African values, and gradually and officially to the replacement of its languages by those of the colonialists. But political independence is now a legal fact. Even if economic independence were potentially within reach, what of cultural independence, autonomy, and identity?†

Cultural identity at both national and international levels remains one of the most basic non-material psychological needs which may well become an increasing source of conflict among and within societies.

---

* The Draft Cultural Charter for Africa, as adopted by the Conference of African Ministers of Culture, Addis Ababa, May 24–27, 1976.

† For one answer to this question, see the report of the Symposium on the "Future Development Prospects of Africa Towards the Year 2000", *op. cit.*, which proposes among other actions programs for "a new pedagogy geared to African unity" and stresses the "need for scientific, cultural, and social values underlying a new approach to development".

The risk of disruption rises as the side effects of historical learning lags begin to be felt. For instance, many Third World decision-makers were, and to a great extent still are, impregnated by the values of the learning systems of the former colonizers.* As they now begin departing from the scene, a new resurgence towards cultural identity is growing. It is the one appeal to which people with or without formal education respond spontaneously. The movements and questions it raises are more critical than any of the financial and economic issues that have halted the North-South dialogues. We are faced with a serious conflict of values. The admission to the "Club of Nation States" has been barred by the resistance of the older members to grant full recognition to the cultural identity of the newer members. There is tolerance but no sincere acceptance of the values of the South because there is no serious effort to understand them. This is what lies at the heart of the failure of the North-South dialogue. Why this value conflict is so fundamental, and why change will have to entail a wide process of individual and societal learning can perhaps best be illustrated by focusing on two issues: the problem of polarization and the impossibility of redistribution.

Cultural identity is an increasing source of international and social conflict.

By the problem of polarization, we mean the intellectual tendency, instilled by our training, to see diversity at the expense of unity, and vice versa. Cultural identity is seen as precluding global interdependence, autonomy as inconsistent with integration, solidarity as a substitute for self reliance, world consciousness as a threat to national independence. The notion of partnership seems to have broken down at the global level. This breakdown is partially a product of learned, or mis-learned, values. We need, for a new learning perspective, a multilateral set of values that sees

The problem of polarization: cultural identity is mistakenly assumed to preclude global interdependence.

---

* As far back as the 14th century, the historian (and sociologist) Ibn Khaldoun described most aptly the phenomenon of mimetism at the level of values between colonizer and colonized in his *Al MuQaddima* (Discourse on Universal History 1377). See also Paul Freire's discussion of how the oppressed strive to imitate the oppressor in *Pedogogy of the Oppressed, op. cit.*

cultural identity for what it is — the opposite of isolationism and withdrawal because it is a prerequisite for meaningful global interaction. The problem consists in learning that the right to diversity implies the necessity for global solidarity. Cultural identity is what gives people dignity, or "not to submit just to survive".

There *does* exist a common cultural heritage of humanity whose enhancement and safekeeping is one of our greatest responsibilities. This heritage can become even more relevant to people if emphasis is put on the human role in its continuous creation* rather than on the museum collections of its artifacts of by-gone times. This outlook that stresses the role of diverse people in creating culture could become the backbone of the concept of "global interdependence". Interdependence does not necessarily require "world government"; but it does imply global comprehension and cooperation, based on a set of ethical norms that prevent sovereignty from becoming cultural aggression.

The immense issues that cultural identity raises are all the more complex because, unlike some material global problems, cultural issues are not resolvable by a process of redistribution. Cultural autonomy is not granted (or withheld) at will through international agreements of redistribution of resources, indispensable as these may be in other cases.

Cultural identity is a problem of learning that is not amenable to international redistribution.

Cultural identity is a perception, a sense of meaning, an integrated context, a set of human relations and values — all of which are proper to learning. A long-term perspective to make these perceptions fully and reciprocally synergetic will be required, because this form of autonomy is conditioned by learning cycles. If we want to prepare a culturally viable 21st century, it would be necessary to begin now to enhance the learning processes of parents *and* of their children who will be reaching adulthood as the 21st century opens.

But how? What do cultural identity, cultural cross-fertilization, and enrichment imply for learning? Two implications may briefly be alluded to. First, the notions of global interdependence through the flourishing of a plurality of cultures exclude the viability of a single

* Values are not static; they are a source for action and change. See P. Kirpal, "The Crisis of Culture and Development" in *Cultures III*, 4, UNESCO, Paris (1976).

universal learning model. Human beings are of one species with a whole universe of common traits, and their learning processes are akin to one another, but each individual or group has their specificity which makes each of them different from one another. This is a hopeful sign to a new learning perspective, if it is taken with seriousness by those whose position and function in the power structure could lead the way to planetary cultural understanding.

Secondly, and finally, what is vital in the process of enhancing cultural identity is the perception of global issues and their complexity. Every person should be able to see these issues from at least two perspectives: from the global view as well as from a culturally specific view, be it national or local. This implies a full respect for the values of others, a consensus on a minimal set of universal values as well as a greater role for international exchanges, carried out on multi-lateral bases, for people of all ages to see the globality of the heritage of humanity from perspectives outside their own culture. The development of this awareness and its dissemination is one of the main objectives for a new learning perspective.

In Conclusion

Epilogue

If one were to extrapolate the current trends — for instance, in the demand for energy, in various economic and trade relations, in the arms race, and in many other conflicts — a gloomy picture emerges for the period to the year 2000 and beyond. Yet ours is not the first generation to live through a time of great changes and dramatic challenges. Our continued survival is testimony that humanity indeed learns. It has successfully threaded its way in and out of disasters, which many look upon as a natural means of acquiring wisdom. But with a dense, highly interconnected population, and possessing a tremendous power for destruction, we are confronted now with the possibility of catastrophic error with unimaginable consequences. Lessons might be created by disaster, but no one might remain to make use of them or the world may be so harmed that the damage is irreparable. So we have to reconsider what is meant by the statement "humanity learns". Does the statement no imply — indeed demand — that learning occur at the right time and on a scale sufficiently large not only to avoid disasters but also to conclude a century, so much traumatized by successive follies, with a gain in peace, dignity, and happiness? Is it beyond our reach to create and choose a way that minimizes suffering?

There are many positive trends visible on the horizon. Governments now meet not only to discuss the classical politics of peace and war, but also to search for solutions to global issues which, until only yesterday, were considered isolated domestic issues but which today are tying us to a common destiny. Great debates are being conducted under the auspices of institutions originally created after World War II to oversee international security. But who would have foreseen that these same institutions would turn their attention, for example, to an International

Year of the Child and that, regardless of differing convictions and creeds, many people would be drawn to examine the destiny of the coming generations?

The new complexities have increased the role of experts, of scientific expertise, and of specialized research studies. These are all indeed necessary. But rapidly dissipating is the myth of the expert who can solve problems more social than technological through technical fixes. Ours is becoming an era of participation. At present, our era is still in the transition phase in which participation lacks adequate understanding and supporting institutions. In the making is a true constituency whose subject is the human impact of global issues and whose experiences and gatherings are workshops for new ideas. Yet debates alone do not solve issues. The key demand is for action. Seldom has the human problematique offered so many opportunities for bold and generous initiatives. This vision is compatible with the perspective offered by innovative learning, which goes beyond the means inherent in simple analysis and decision or in conventional technologies and organizations. It draws its resources from wide participation and from looking to the future.

A new decade of development is being launched by the United Nations. It must take into account the lessons of the two preceding decades of development which saw an overemphasis on economic expertise. What could be more challenging than for all people to join the renewed efforts aimed at narrowing the gaps which divide humanity, focusing our energies towards a peaceful, profoundly human, enterprise?

If we consider development as a process of learning, many assumptions long taken for granted fade away. For instance, the issue of development is global. It cannot, as conceived in the past, concern only a part of humanity. All countries have a stake in development, from whichever perspective it may be seen. It would be a gross error if a privileged minority, preoccupied with its own concerns, were to look with indifference on the struggle of others seeking solutions to their acute problems – as if the concerns of part of the world are not related to the problems of others.

The innovative learning perspective does not focus on a pattern so familiar to managers of local or larger organizations, of fixing objectives, marshalling resources, and initiating methods of implementation. In the context of innovative learning, objectives, resources, and methods are all subject to change. The manner in which they are linked may be more important than their operation. The human factor is more central and predominant than the problem to be solved. The development and unfolding of human potential is what ultimately determines the success or failure of economic, social, or any other kind of development.

A good strategy for formulating and evaluating action in the coming decades should center on how many obstacles impeding participation have been removed, and how many alternative options have been opened up by an anticipatory approach. The prevailing criteria based on short term economic success seem increasingly to be leading to triumphs quickly followed by new and irremedial difficulties. No process can be judged successful when it leads to solutions that induce further and more severe problems.

Recent currents of thought have provided clear indications that development should foster self-reliance, meet basic human needs, and promote harmony with nature. And we would add — ensure human development. A wide international context of global cooperation based on humanistic values is essential for this type of development.

A report such as this one on learning must be open-ended. Had it proposed any fixed formulas, it would have been self-defeating. Instead, the publication of this report is intended to be an invitation to reflect on some basic assumptions and concepts, and to stimulate discussion and debate among concerned people everywhere about learning and humanity's future.

Authors' Commentary on the Learning Project

Debates about the Problematique and the Human Element

The emphasis on the human element as central to the global problematique does not originate with this report or with those concerned primarily with learning. Our own views grow out of several significant movements that began towards the mid-seventies, two of which are cited here as examples. One centers on meeting basic human needs*

---

* See John and Magda McHale, *Basic Human Needs*, Transition Books, 1978; or A.Herrera, H. D. Scolnik *et al.*, *op. cit.*

and another on the search for a consensus about the goals* of humanity. Both provide significant approaches and continue to be the subject of stimulating discussion. It has not been possible, however, to ascertain an agreed-upon list of needs or goals on which to build a universal outlook. Except for cases where inadequate food, health, or shelter leads to needless waste of human life itself, the panorama of needs and goals is a shifting one that varies with time and differs according to the cultural perspective of the viewer. Indeed, some Third World observers feel that the cause of basic human needs has become politicized to the point where lack of progress in this field is used as a pretext for denying further international cooperation for development.

We do not see innovative learning as contradictory to these earlier approaches; indeed, we hope it extends them. Learning may provide a dynamic aspect to the basic needs and goals approaches insofar as ways of recognizing, meeting, and re-defining basic needs have to be learned; and means for re-orienting, broadening, and reaching consensus on goals also entail learning. Moreover, despite the fact that the methods for and commitment to innovative learning are still at present underdeveloped, learning is a subject area that promises to provide a basis for mutual cooperation and dialogue among East and West, North and South.

Recent Debates about Learning and Education

Raising questions about the adequacy of maintenance learning has recent precedents, starting most notably in the controversial events of the 1960s. What was called the "crisis of education" — typified by the student protests that began in Berkeley in 1964 and that were followed by the "spirit of contesting" in Paris in 1968 — is one among several examples of periodic revolts against an over-predominance of maintenance learning. Many of these protests, misconstrued by some as a problem solely of "generation gap", were aimed at the rigid structural

* For example, see Ervin Laszlo *et al.*, *Goals for Mankind, A Report to The Club of Rome on the New Horizons of Global Community*, E.P. Dutton, 1977. Also see Saul Mendlovitz (ed.), *On the Creation of a Just World Order*, The Free Press, 1975.

impediments in educational systems and in society as a whole.

The events of the sixties helped to launch several important studies which are antecedents to this report, such as the one conducted by the International Commission established by UNESCO and directed by Edgar Faure.* Another which appeared at the height of the protests was a worldwide study by Philip H. Coombs on *The World Educational Crisis*.† In other studies, the discontent and challenge was so great that some people reached the extreme of questioning not only the usefulness but even the right to existence of the school establishment.‡

In response to these events, many countries introduced educational reforms that followed one another in a seemingly endless parade whose progress became increasingly dissipated with the passing of time. New concepts, chief among them lifelong learning, open education, modular curricula, and a variety of methods supported by educational technology, were introduced but only sporadically accepted. Nevertheless, this spirit of contesting the established structures drew the attention of the world, at least for a brief poignant moment, to the shortcomings of educational systems dominated by an excessive concern for maintenance learning.

What remains today of this spirit of the sixties? Not only has the wave of questioning and experimentation receded; at present, one senses a dangerous mood of reaction and a retrenchment against innovation. Ten years after the 1968 events of Paris, some publications celebrate the failures of reform with short-sighted jubilation. The reaction to the contesting of maintenance learning is in danger of leading to an overreaction or backlash against all forms of innovative learning. At a time when the global issues demand a type of learning that encourages renewal and restructuring, the trend is to cling to maintenance learning and reject innovative learning. If there is a lesson to be learned from the crisis of education in the sixties and the concern for global issues in the seventies, it is the realization that the two are linked, not only to

---

⁑ *Learning to Be: The World of Education Today and Tomorrow,* a report by the International Commission on the Development of Education, Edgar Faure *et al.,* UNESCO, Paris, 1972.

† Philip H. Coombs, *The World Educational Crisis: A Systems Analysis,* Oxford University Press, 1968.

‡ See *Deschooling Society,* Ivan Illich, Harrow Books, 1970.

each other, but to the macro-issue of the role of the human element as cause of and potential solution to the world problematique.

Learning and the Problematique in the Eighties

Looking ahead to the decade of the 1980s, there is little question that it will be a decade of learning. The 1979 U.N. world conferences on the Application of Science and Technology for Development (UNCSTD), Trade and Development (UNCTAD V), and on Agrarian Reform and Rural Development — as well as the special sessions of the U.N. General Assembly devoted to assessing progress on the New International Economic Order (1980) and on Disarmament (1981 or 1982) — are pivotal examples of the turning points we face. Frustration with inaction is building. Humanity either learns ways to reverse the arms race, or invites an era of shock incalculably more dreadful. The North and South either learn to restructure the international order co-operatively, or commence a period inescapably more combative and crisis-prone. The question is not *whether* the eighties will usher in learning, but *what kind* of learning the decade is bringing. Will humanity be taught by shocks, whose lessons entail prohibitive costs and deadly delays, or will people learn how to shape those events which with intelligence and willpower could be controlled? Will the preoccupation with maintenance learning lead to a type of learning imposed by events, or can humanity consciously develop and practice a type of innovative learning appropriate to a world of between four and six billion diverse people faced with current and future global issues?

Some Personal Observations on the Learning Project

Trilateral dialogues are an enriching experience, especially when they are to be translated into a common stand in a written form. For the three co-authors, this project has been a laboratory for the testing of mutual tolerance, international communication, and the quest for universality within irreducible differences. Coming from dissimilar cultures, being familiar with the social realities known as East, West,

North, and South, we have learned the importance of listening to new arguments and of shedding the narrow outlooks of disciplines in which we have been separately trained. We believe we have acquired insights which we could not have attained individually. While this collective undertaking has been for us a source of strength, we are nonetheless fully conscious of the weaknesses which will be evident to readers in terms of the flow and expression of ideas. We have become aware, however, of just how deeply the human gap cuts across all cultures, values, ideologies, races, and religions. Debate and discussion about the human gap and its relation to the world problematique necessarily calls for an international dialogue on the need for commitment to and practice of innovation if we wish to ensure the universal vision required to enhance both the diversity of cultures and the common global requirements for survival and dignity.

Comments by Participants of the Salzburg Conference on Learning (June, 1979)

In June, 1979, The Club of Rome convened a conference in Salzburg, Austria, opened by Dr. Rudolf Kirchschlaeger, President of the Republic of Austria and attended by 150 participants, who were welcomed by Dr. Wilfried Haslauer, Governor of the Province of Salzburg, Dr. Willibald Pahr, Federal Minister for Foreign Affairs, and Heinrich Salfenauer, Mayor of the city of Salzburg. The authors of the *Learning Report* presented their findings, and many of the comments and suggestions made during the Salzburg meeting were subsequently incorporated into the final text.

The conference also revealed a wealth of ideas which were discussed during the course of three workshops. Summaries of these workshops are presented below.

SUMMARY OF WORKSHOP I: LEARNING AND GLOBAL ISSUES

Chairmen: Romesh Thapar (India)
Ervin Laszlo (USA)
Rapporteur: Carlos Mallmann (Argentina)

The *Learning Report* certainly created in this workshop one of its main desired effects: it provoked and catalyzed thinking about how learning is linked to global issues. There were many words of both praise and constructive criticism. A number of common fundamental concerns and viewpoints emerged during the discussions. The main reactions of the participants are briefly summarized below.

Learning is a personal and social as well as an environmental activity – i.e., it encompasses *intra*-human, *inter*-human, and *extra*-human aspects which may be seen as *inputs* and as *outputs* operating in one or more *contexts*. From an input point of view, participants stressed the need to distinguish between conventional and creative learning – that is, between *know how* and *know why*.

From an output perspective, this normative "know-why" learning should be focused on the social aims of enhancing the quality of life and on the individual or personal goals of human growth and self-actualization. As for the contexts of learning, participants felt that more emphasis has to be given to the cultural aspects of the dialogues about the world problematique – especially the need for cultural identity and the role of the rural poor in the Third World.

Other contextual considerations focused on the need to consider not only rational, logical thought but also intuitive, "analogic" thinking; not only personal but also societal learning; and not just centralized plans and structures, but rather the small decentralized actions that could be taken.

Some of the most crucial global issues in which learning was a particularly significant factor were identified and discussed. These included rural poverty, food and nutrition, the arms race, illiteracy, urban over-concentration, energy, communication – particularly the impact of the "telectronics revolution" – and the various effects deriving from the misuse of political power. The stress was put on alternative perspectives of the world problematique. The participants felt that the report should stress learning for the eradication of *poverty* – not only material poverty but also the poverties of understanding, of security and protection, of love and compassion, of autonomy and anticipation, of meaning and spiritual justice, and of equity.

A major goal for innovative learning should be explicitly stated: to combat and transform the norms that encourage the maximization of material consumption, the concentration of power, and the continuation of ways of life that are competitive, antagonistic, alienating, and unduly exploitative of nature – all of the norms which are part of the predominant paradigm of "modern industrial society". Special reference was made to the urgent need to bring learning to bear on the universal problem of rigid social and mental structures that lead to paternalistic, authoritarian, male-dominated relationships.

Unlike material poverty, this poverty in understanding, values, and learning cannot be said to be concentrated mainly in developing countries. For example, the lack of effective participation and intuitive understanding – a scarcity of love, as someone expressed it – are widespread in the so-called "developed" countries. This clearly points to the need for reevaluating the norms of Western cultures and encouraging societal learning through increased dialogue among and within cultures, sub-cultures, and different social groups. The *Université des Mutants* in Senegal was cited as an example of action taken in this direction; it was also suggested that the United Nations University should devote more of its efforts toward these aims.

An important part of the workshop discussion dealt with the obstacles which stand in the way of effective solutions to global problems and with the impediments to the furthering of alternatives for proposed solutions. A distinction was made between the need and possibilities for accelerating learning processes of decision-makers at all levels of institutional learning, on the one hand, and the equally urgent necessity but greater difficulty of enhancing the more general and slower processes of societal or "public" learning, on the other. One suggestion to up-grade broad-based societal learning was to focus on the already existing universal concern for the future that parents, especially mothers, feel for their children. More stress needs to be put on "inventing the future" to ensure that human development receives a high priority.

Action by the Government of Venezuela

The President of Venezuela, Dr. Luis Herrera Campins, at the very beginning of his term in March 1979, appointed as Minister of State for the development of human intelligence Dr. Luis Alberto Machado, author of *The Revolution of Intelligence* and "The Right to be Intelligent",* and who appears in the Partial List of Participants at Learning Project Conferences (see p. 140).

With this "anticipatory" initiative the government of Venezuela aims – according to Minister Machado's statements at the Salzburg Conference of The Club of Rome in June 1979 – to put into practice the principles that appear in this report. The act of President Herrera

* To be published by Pergamon Press, Oxford, in 1980.

is a good example of a political decision that governments could take in order to bring awareness and concern to increasing numbers of the people of the world about the learning problematique and find ways and means to solve it.

SUMMARY OF WORKSHOP II: ENHANCING LEARNING IN
CONTEMPORARY SOCIETY

Chairmen: Adam Schaff (Poland)
Ricardo Díez Hochleitner (Spain)
Rapporteur: Eleonora Barbieri Masini (Italy)

The part of the discussion of Workshop II relating to the methodology of the report suggested a need

● For more precision in terminology as well as the concepts it describes. For example, literacy is not clearly related to interlinking parameters such as inequality. Other examples of concepts that need further clarification are anticipatory and participatory learning as well as conventional and non-conventional learning. In the course of the meeting, however, some definitions of these and other terms seemed to emerge.

● For more concreteness in the examples. It was felt that Part IV on "Illustrations of a New Learning Perspective" did not reflect the expectations emerging in the preceding three parts.

● For the report to be expressed in a more innovative manner. This would take into account the means at our disposal beyond the written word, especially the mass media. Indeed, partly due to the Salzburg meeting, plans are underway to explore the feasibility of explaining innovative learning concepts via television.

● For thinking in terms of "desirables" as well as "possibles". It was deemed desirable to propose a project for the future in terms of innovative learning, even though the concrete outcome might not presently be predictable with precision.

Another part of the discussion relating to the objectives and content of the report stressed

● On the one hand, the socio-political context of learning is not sufficiently present in the report, which is mainly a "left side of the brain" (or rational/systematic) presentation that stresses a politically loaded interpretation based on the developed-developing concepts. Learning should also be understood and linked to an interpretation different from this traditional systemic one. One should consider the Third World and industrialized poor as opposed to the developed rich and dominant classes in the Third World.

● What is especially important and currently lacking is "socio-political will". This lack is a greater problem for learning than the capacity to cope with complexity as cited in the report.

The learning project should aim at helping those who are committed to change in order to influence institutions where the presence of power and resources are accompanied by an absence of political will. The report should aim at making explicit the implicit values of educational structures supporting the dominant powers.

● On the other hand, there was a request for a minimal value consensus which should be achievable in the present historical moment. For example, we should be able to agree at least on "the right to education".

● Between these two positions, an interesting concept was presented — the need for *limits to diversity*. Where are such limits and by what procedures can they be identified and agreed upon?

● Finally, an additional point was stressed that in the report there seems to be an underlying assumption that global issues can be *resolved* by innovative societal learning. Society, however, is inherently conflictual and hence global issues are not "resolvable" in some final sense but need to be seen as conflictual.

As guidelines for the group discussion on how to encourage a new learning perspective, participants took the report's four main examples — literacy, work and education, the role of the university, and the mass media. For each of these areas, the discussions covered both some basic conceptual elements that should be added or re-emphasized in the report as well as strategies for implementing these.

1. *Literacy*

● Literacy is a problem not only of the developing world but also of the developed world.

● "Aesthetic literacy": The concept of literacy has to be expanded to include the use of images or of those aesthetic values related to the quality of life.

● Literacy does not relate merely to the "three R's" and to formal schooling but also to the informal sector outside of schooling. As part of learning in general, literacy can no longer be restricted to artificial boundaries.

● Literacy must relate – in addition to the social, economic and political environment – to the population element. The three elements most directly connected to literacy are work, education, and population. This third element is a strategic one. It is not only a question of absolute numbers but of relating literacy to the entire population, especially to the working population.

● Drop-outs and "literacy relapse" – as well as the obverse possibility of regaining literacy where it has been lost – are strong indicators of the severity or resilience of a society's literacy condition.

● In conclusion, literacy has to be thought of in non-conventional terms. Such thinking is like considering a "problem within a problem", or, as one participant put it, "dissonance within cognitive dissonance".

Several suggestions were offered for strategic recommendations:

● Literacy has to make people *productive* in their own environment (this definition of literacy seems to have received the group's consensus).

● Literacy has to be evaluated in terms of both material and non-material costs. Literacy is expensive, especially if it provokes alienation from one's original culture. Losing a traditional culture is a case in point in many developing countries where the language question becomes an especially critical one.

2. *Work and Education*

● Questions of work and education differ in the context industrialized or Third World societies. The concept of leisure, for example, is not the same in mostly urban industrial countries as it is in mostly rural Third World countries, where it is seen in a different time perspective. The concept of leisure is also differentiated by class and regional distinctions.

● On the other hand, one can foresee the emergence of societies where further automation and a revolution in micro-processing will provoke more and more unemployment. A social catastrophe with far-reaching changes is impending, and replacements for "work" defined in conventional terms must be sought.

● Unemployment and marginalization – especially among youth, women, and workers – are growing in many of the industrialized societies. The phenomenon is linked to many elements of the dichotomy between work and education, among which the following were indicated: formal education is identified as a way of escaping manual work; evaluation of workers is made at the school level for economic reasons; working in school for external, social reasons rather than internal individual reasons is predominant; no stage of formal education is complete with its own profile, always needing a next step; formal education encompasses the hidden values of any given society.

The strategies discussed were

● The proposal in the report for an average of one day per week outside school makes sense only in cultures where children or youth do not already have to work. Further, the timing aspect would have to be modified, for example, in places such as in rural Sri Lanka or in Kenya where programs have already been implemented. In these cases, children work in community development education on farms where school terms are related to seasons.

● Vocational training outside the educational system is being tried in Spain where it is also related to opportunities for old people.

● Nationally sponsored incentives to take advantage of learning opportunities in agriculture in Sri Lanka and India were cited as good examples of integrating work and education.

3. The Role of the University

● Despite rhetoric to the contrary, primary schools have not yet reached their enrolment targets while universities have exceeded theirs, even though financially each university student costs an average of nearly fifty times more than each primary school pupil.

● Although a main university objective is to conduct research, universities often do not answer the research needs of the community where they are located because of their separation from reality. As a result, applied research often takes place outside universities in other, usually private, institutions.

● Especially in countries still undergoing the process of decoloniazation, the "reincarnation" of university models derived from the developed world demonstrates the extent of the divorce between the university and its local surroundings. In developing countries in general, this divorce is reinforced by the dichotomy between universities and politics which has often led to frustrations and losses of academic freedom.

● Many universities are not prone to change. In Egypt, the current doubling time for university students is every five years while for teachers it is every fifteen years. This is one small sign of possible rigidity. On the other hand, it was also noted that universities can strengthen national identity.

Some of the strategies for universities were:

● Financing university programs was thought to be an increasingly important concern. Universities may have to prove they can face community problems in order to successfully secure funds from government agencies and foundations.

● Natural sciences in the university can be aided at the international level more easily than humanities, which can best be developed at national levels.

● Universities should deal with global problems.

● Finally, universities should take the leadership in indicating the outlines for political action.

4. Mass Media

● An impending revolution in new electronic technologies was stressed as being already with us and here to stay. Microprocessors can be a motor for further diversity in learning but they could lead also to a reinforcement of conventional thinking and values.

● The relation between television and the domination of national and international powers was emphasized. A clear example is the scarcity of minorities on most national TV programs.

● For developing countries, radio is the most widespread medium. Rural workers have access to it, listening to music and drama while working. Here educational programs can be inserted and used, as is the case in Sri Lanka.

Some of the strategies for the mass media were:

● What is needed is not the production of more information but its dissemination to where it is needed.

● A worldwide evaluation of the social consequences of the various media should be made, for its importance to learning may be considerable.

● Leading papers, radio, and television representatives from all over the world should be invited to attend a seminar on "innovative learning and the role of the media", since the communications media are directly related to the perceptions of the public.

● A joint international effort should be set up to dedicate at least one-fifth of every organization's capacity *toward doing something innovatively*. To this aim a seminar, under Club of Rome leadership, could be prepared and the "human gap" issue could be debated in depth.

● Children's television was cited as a special case where an analysis should be launched to find guidelines for a code of conduct that can be used for legislative purposes.

SUMMARY OF WORKSHOP III: LEARNING RESEARCH

Chairmen: Mohammed Kassas (Egypt)
Donald Michael (USA)
Rapporteur: Raoul Kneucker (Austria)

Statement of Purposes

If Workshops I and II were concerned with creating a new public awareness and with convincing our fellow citizens and our political leaders to translate the report into reality, Workshop III was concerned with continuing the work through additional research, studies, and projects that would help to implement the report's proposals.

The section of the report on learning research, pp. 100-102, was generally supported and, indeed, served as a basis for the discussions; at the same time, it was considered too short and not specific enough.

Should there be more research at all? Relevant research has been done, studies and reform projects, particularly by international organizations, have been carried out and were neglected or frustrated.

The participants did not overestimate the possible effects of science and research in linking political decision-making with insights into global problems; they agreed, however, that there is a need for new research and for new research efforts:

● Learning research should take new directions and should include new aspects; for there are still blank spots on the map of scientific exploration of human learning.

● Learning research should be re-oriented, interdisciplinarity should help to overcome the detrimental "sovereignty" of the individual disciplines.

● Many projects will be necessary to apply available and future research, to stimulate acceptance of research results, and to campaign successfully for a "New International, or rather *Global*, Learning Order".

We felt it a moral obligation to propose new research efforts, even if it were without the hope of meeting the global challenges in time.

Interdisciplinarity

The "world problematique" is mirrored in learning theories and research. Many disciplines are engaged in learning research, progressing individually but disregarding each other's results. Biochemistry, the neuro-sciences, several streams of psychology, the educational sciences, communication research, linguistics, political science, organizational theory, public administration, and international relations contribute to the growing yet stifling complexity.

Three "schools of thought" may be distinguished: one using formal, mathematical, and cybernetic approaches, with learning machines, artificial intelligence, and computers, neglecting values and motifs; another one employing biological, physiological, and neurological approaches, unable to explain meanings and to help understand contexts and frames of references; a third one using different psychological approaches, without putting the human beings in the center, studying rather their natural history instead of their human qualities and inter-dependences. In effect, each of these schools is reductionist, and con-tributes to re-inforcing the existing behavioral patterns, values, and systems. Their orientation is adaptive rather than anticipatory.

In the history of science, specialization and disciplinary fragmentation are not an unprecedented situation; synthesis always followed. Today, global issues necessitate again an integration of scientific disciplines.

Our plea for interdisciplinarity does not pay lip-service to this notion. The following proposals are intended to make interdisciplinarity operational in learning research:

● The plan for a "Yearbook" or quarterly on learning should soon be implemented; a scholarly publication will provide a public forum for debate and for confrontation of various fields. Its editors and reviewers must be charged with the tasks of stimulating com-parisons and encouraging interdisciplinary studies.

● Regular international interdisciplinary conferences and work-shops can be helpful for discussion, exchange, and presentation of learning research, but will be insufficient.

● We ask the Club of Rome to propose to UNESCO an inter-national Programme on Learning, in format and volume comparable to UNISIST and MAB.

Research Issues and Research Areas

The participants will certainly be asked by many a sceptic what aspects of the report can be translated into reality (although the proper question would be, What should be translated and in which order?). They can answer:

● They found the new ideas and terms of the report "contagious", and communicating them seemed easy to them.

● The key notions of the report — anticipatory and participatory learning — are operational in themselves, for, taken seriously, they mean that teaching and learning can start now applying or practicing them. Parents, teachers, managers, administrators, political leaders — in short, all educators — can immediately adopt new attitudes and change their present behavior.

● In particular, teacher training can confirm or re-establish the role of the teacher, today often a specialist and a mere instructor, as an intelligent and moral example for the student, as a catalyst and a manager of the student's learning process, teaching how to learn and how to participate. Audio-visual aids and learning machines constitute unconvincing instruments for teaching and learning, for they do not challenge creativity or participation, although they might help the teachers to speed up or increase the volume of learning. Into learning, specifically into formal education, the joy of learning, of life-long learning as a human way to development, must be re-introduced, purpose and sense of learning must be instilled again.

Individual Learning ("Micro-learning")

Workshop III stated that "maintenance learning" could not and should not be replaced by "innovative learning". Learning will have to still rely on trial and error, and adaptive learning will continue to be both practical and necessary; on the contrary, maintenance learning should also be improved in order to better prepare for future crises. However, conventional forms of learning are less and less effective today, and we must accelerate our capabilities for innovative learning and we must find a new balance between new and traditional forms of learning.

Future research might clarify the human learning process. Today, we are only able to answer the less ambitious question: How can we improve our learning, i.e. change the posture of learning; learn to re-examine, to re-perceive, to re-formulate, and to re-learn; create new alternatives and change patterns of thinking and frames of references?

Innovative modes of learning will be promoted by

- Comparative studies, in many fields;
- Cross-national studies;
- Studies in the philosophy of science;
- Future studies, simulation games, case studies, scenarios;
- Communication research;
- Tutorial learning.

Innovative learning must not be misconstrued as merely a new technique, simply to be added to the existing curricula. It involves the total human being. Anticipatory and participatory learning requires holistic approaches. Learning must again affect the intellect, the emotions, and the will power of humans. Today, education is intellect biased. Old ideals of education are often neglected in daily practice. Fantasy, creativity — on which both science and the arts are based — solidarity, tolerance, and empathy are affective qualilities which must be developed and exercised as well as will power, decision-making, and participation. Students must experience to participate, must learn to integrate work and life, to develop critical faculties, to apply new knowledge and implement new ideas, and to change their way of life.

Collective/Societal Learning ("Macro-learning")

Much research has been done on individual learning processes; hardly any research is done on organizational or group or societal learning. This is clearly a new research area.

In the management sciences only, organizational learning is being studied and its improvement is being attempted. But do groups or societies learn similarly? How do they learn to change? What are, in fact, their articulation processes? Political science today concerns itself with the "documentation" of politics more than with the societal learning that precedes it. It seems quite evident that "maintenance learning" also describes societal learning adequately — alternatives still come through shocks and other impulses from outside.

Major tasks for research lie ahead. How should organizations, both private and public, the groups and the society as a whole be structured to allow learning procedures to happen and to create an atmosphere conducive to learning, to secure free articulation, and to accept alternatives? What will be the design of the future institutions of learning?

Salzburg Conference: Closing Remarks

At the closing session, the Deputy Director General of UNESCO, Dr. Federico Mayor, expressed his agreement with the suggestions made in the report concerning the launching of a major international interdisciplinary research project on learning. He said:

"The UNESCO response to the plea contained in the *Learning Report* for the launching of an international learning research project similar to the ones that UNESCO has undertaken for the biosphere (MAB) or for scientific and technological information (UNISIST) is very good. Let us now study jointly and in depth what concrete follow-up actions can be identified and undertaken. I feel strongly that the time has now come to proceed to feasibility studies. This is indeed the only response on the part of UNESCO I can imagine. This initiative by The Club of Rome for the further development of the concept of learning, placing learning in the position of the central phenomenon of new societies, is a most timely and fundamental one.

"I consider the report valuable because it refers to learning as the means of closing the human gap, and because it centres development on Man, an approach to world problems which is shared by UNESCO; and I fully endorse the proposal for a concerted approach to the different issues raised by the report.

"In 1972 the general conference of UNESCO was presented with the report entitled *Learning to Be* — in its French version *Apprendre à Être* — reminiscent of the French title of *No Limits to Learning, Apprendre à Devenir.* The gist of its message was to propose lifelong education as the master concept for educational policies in the years to come for both developed and developing countries. Implicit in the report was the idea that education should prepare for types of societies yet to come, for models which do not yet exist, preparing the way for permanent, life-long, anticipatory education; with the major goal of introducing 'the learning society'.

"But the time has come to go further. What can or what should individual learning be in order for the individual to be able to cope with the increasing complexity of life, to face the future of the human condition? The time is ripe for studies and research of a forward-looking nature, and the general conference of UNESCO at its twentieth session last year approved the long-term programme for reflection on the future development of education (education in the year 2000).

"It is worth recalling here that we are living in a world of about 900 million illiterates, of an even greater number of sick and hungry, a world in which hundreds of millions are deprived of elementary human rights. At the same time, in the same world, the amount spent annually on armaments is about 450 thousand million dollars, or almost 1.5 thousand million a day. With only a fraction of these resources, most of the global problems of mankind could be seriously tackled. The resources exist, but they are being used for the 'other alternative' − that of devoting sixty times more money to a soldier than to a student. The wrong alternative is being followed, and the shift to the right one requires a world-wide mobilization and, in the first place, the necessary political will."

Salzburg, June 1979   **Federico Mayor**

Salzburg Conference Rapporteurs

The rapporteurs for the overall conference were Donald Lesh (USA) and Roberto Vacca (Italy).

Partial List of Participants
at Learning Project Conferences

GYÖRGY ADAMS, Eötvös Lorand University, Budapest, Hungary

UVAIS AHAMED, Asian Institute for Broadcasting Development, UNESCO Regional Broadcasting Office, Kuala Lumpur, Malaysia (Sri Lanka*)

ABDUL MALIK AL HAMMAR, Managing Director, United Arab Emirates Currency Board, Abu Dhabi, UAE

DWIGHT ALLEN, Education Research Center, Old Dominion University, Virginia, USA

SERGE ANTOINE, Ministry of the Environment and the Quality of Life, Paris, France

M. K. ANTWI, Cape Coast University, Cape Coast, Ghana

JACK AUSTIN, Harvard Business School and EDUCOM, Cambridge, Mass., USA

SEVERIO AVVEDUTO, Director General, Ministry of Public Education, Rome, Italy

CHADLY AYARI, Arab Bank for the Economic Development of Africa, Paris, France

DUNCAN BALLANTINE, World Bank Education Division, Washington, D.C., USA

ESTABAN SÁNCHEZ BARCIA, journalist, El País, Madrid, Spain

JUDITH BARNET, Judith Barnet Associates, Barnstable, Mass., USA

AMINA BELRHITI, University Mohamed V, Rabat, Morocco

ABDELLATIF BENABDELJALIL, Rector, University Mohamed V, Rabat, Morocco

DRISS BENSARI, University Mohamed V, Rabat, Morocco

MIHAI BOTEZ, Systems Studies Division, University of Bucharest, Bucharest, Romania

* Indicates nationality where different from place of work.

CARSTEN BRESCH, Institute for Genetics, Freiburg, Federal Republic of Germany

GERHART BRUCKMANN, International Institute of Applied Systems Analysis, Laxenburg, Austria

JAMES BURGWYN, West Chester State University, Philadelphia, Pennsylvania, USA

MANUEL CALVO HERNANDO, Asociación Iberoamericana de Periodistas Científicas, Madrid, Spain

PAUL CAMOUS, Ministry of Education, Paris, France

CLAUDIO deMOURA CASTRO, ECIEL, Rio de Janeiro, Brazil

GEORGE CHRISTIE, International Center for Integrative Studies, New York, USA

PAULO da COSTA MOURA, *Journal do Brasil*, Rio de Janeiro, Brazil

KENNETH DADZIE, Director General for Development and International Economic Cooperation, United Nations, New York (Ghana*)

JOSÉ DELGADO, Director, Departamento de Investigación, Centro Ramón y Cajal, Madrid, Spain

HENRI DIEUZEIDE, Director, Structures, Contents, Methods, and Techniques of Education Division, UNESCO, Paris, France

AMBASSADOR DÍEZ ALEGRIA, Ministry of Foreign Affairs, Madrid, Spain

RICARDO DÍEZ-HOCHLEITNER, Director, Fundación General Mediterránea, Madrid, Spain

ELIZABETH DODSON GRAY, Bolton Institute, Wellesley, Mass., USA

AFSANE EGHBAL, ethnologist, Paris, France (Iran*)

ADEMOLA EKULONA, television producer, Philadelphia, Pennsylvania, USA

THOMAS H. ELIOT, former Chancellor, Washington University, St. Louis, Missouri, USA

ABDEL AZIZ HAMED EL-KOUSSY, Ain Shams University, Cairo, Egypt

LILLIAN ESSELSTYN, The Caldwell B. Esselstyn Foundation, Claverack, New York, USA

MAX FIGUEROA, Vice Prime Minister's Office, Havana, Cuba

* Indicates nationality where different from place of work.

JOHN FOBES, Duke University, Chapel Hill, North Carolina, USA
ALOYSIUS FONSECA, Civiltà Cattolica, Rome, Italy
BERNARD FORTIN, International Labour Office (ILO), Geneva, Switzerland
GABRIEL FRAGNIÈRE, European Foundation for Culture, Brussels, Belgium (Switzerland*)
BRUNO FRITSCH, Eidgenoessische Technische Hochschule, Zurich, Switzerland
ROGER GARAUDY, Institut International pour le Dialogue des Civilisations, Chennevières-sur-Marne, France
J. R. GASS, OECD, Paris, France
MIHNEA GHEORGHIU, President, Académie des Sciences Sociales et Politiques, Bucharest, Romania
ORIO GIARINI, Secretary General, Association Internationale pour l'Étude de l'Économie de l'Assurance, Geneva, Switzerland
MAURICE GUERNIER, member, The Club of Rome, Paris, France
JOHN A. HARRIS IV, Chairman, U.S. Association for The Club of Rome, Philadelphia, Pennsylvania, USA
BOHDAN HAWRYLYSHYN, Centre d'Études Industrielles, Geneva, Switzerland
HAZEL HENDERSON, Office of Technology Assessment, Congress of the United States, Washington, D.C., USA
SIGURD HÖLLINGER, Federal Ministry of Science and Research, Vienna, Austria
GERHARD HUBER, Präsident des Schweizerischen Wissenschaftesrates, Zurich, Switzerland
TORSTEN HUSÉN, Institute of International Education, University of Stockholm, Stockholm, Sweden
SHOGO ICHIKAWA, National Institute for Educational Research, Tokyo, Japan
T. RAND IDE, Chairman, Ontario Education Communication Authority, Toronto, Canada
MARIUS IOSIFESCU, Center of Mathematical Statistics, Bucharest, Romania

Indicates nationality where different from place of work..

HUGUES DE JOUVENEL, Director, Association Internationale Futuribles, Paris, France

STANE JUŽNIĆ, University of Ljubljana, Ljubljana, Yugoslavia

MOHAMMED KASSAS, University of Cairo, Cairo, Egypt

CHERYL HOLLMANN KEEN, Harvard University, Cambridge, Mass., USA

JAMES P. KEEN, Harvard University, Cambridge, Mass., USA

CLARK KERR, Carnegie Council in Policy Studies in Higher Education, Berkeley, California, USA

SHEIK AMIDOU KHANE, Ministre de Développement Industriel, Senegal

ALEXANDER KING, Chairman, International Federation of Institutes for Advanced Study, Paris, France

BORIS KLUCHNIKOV, Director, Educational Policy and Planning Division, UNESCO, Paris, France (USSR*)

RAOUL KNEUCKER, Austrian University Rectors Conference, Vienna, Austria

RUDOLF KNOEPFEL, The Solvay American Corporation, New York, USA

CARDINAL FRANZ KOENIG, Archbishop of Vienna, Vienna, Austria

ARINA KOWNER, Fédération des Coopératives Migros, Zurich, Switzerland

RANJIT KUMAR, Executive Director, Foundation for International Training for Third World Countries, Don Mills, Canada

TAHAR LABIB, University of Tunis, Tunis, Tunisia

ABDELJALIL LAHJOMRI, Director, École Normale Supérieure, Rabat, Morocco

SHEILA LANE, Harvard University, Cambridge, Mass., USA

CHAKIB LAROUSSI, journalist, Maghreb Arab Press (MAP), Rabat, Morocco

ERVIN LASZLO, Special Fellow, UNITAR, New York, USA

PABLO LATAPÍ, Prospectiva Universitaria, Mexico City, Mexico

DONALD LESH, Executive Director, U.S. Association for The Club of Rome, Washington, D.C., USA

---

* Indicates nationality where different from place of work.

HANS ADAM VON LIECHTENSTEIN, Schloss Vaduz, Vaduz, Liechtenstein

GREGORIO LOPEZ BRAVO, Ingeniero Naval; member, Board of Directors, Spanish Association for The Club of Rome, Madrid, Spain

LUIS ALBERTO MACHADO, Minister of State for the Development of Human Intelligence, Venezuela

MIHAELA MALITZA, Central Institute for Informatics, Bucharest, Romania

ROBERT MALLET, Rector, University of Paris, Paris, France

CARLOS MALLMANN, Executive President, Bariloche Foundation, Buenos Aires, Argentina

GINO MARTINOLI, Centro Studi Investimento Sociali, Rome, Italy

ELEONORA BARBIERI MASINI, Secretary General, World Future Studies Federation, Rome, Italy

ROBERT MAXWELL, Chairman, Pergamon Press, Oxford, U.K.

JOSÉ ANTONIO MAYOBRE, Central Bank of Venezuela, Caracas, Venezuela

FEDERICO MAYOR ZARAGOZA, Deputy Director General, UNESCO, Paris, France

DEONATUS MBILIMA, Prime Minister's Office, Dar-es-Salaam, Tanzania

J. F. McDOUGALL, Director, International Year of the Child, European Secretariat, Geneva, Switzerland

MAGDA McHALE, Center for Integrated Studies, University of Houston, Houston, Texas, USA

DONALD MICHAEL, University of Michigan, Ann Arbor, Michigan, USA

EDWARD MORGAN, radio journalist, *Atlantic Dateline*, Washington, D.C., USA

JENS NAUMANN, Max Planck Institute for Pedagogical Research, Berlin, Federal Republic of Germany

GRIGORE NICOLA, Institute of Pedagogical and Psychological Research, Bucharest, Romania

EDMOND NICOLAU, Polytechnical Institute, Bucharest, Romania

PIETER NOUWEN, journalist, *Elseviers Weekblad,* Amsterdam, Netherlands

JOSÉ MANUEL OTERO NOVAS, Minister of Education, Madrid, Spain

SABURO OKITA, Chairman, Japan Economic Research Center, Tokyo, Japan

IONITZA OLTEANU, Editor, *Revista Economica*, Bucharest, Romania

WILLEM OLTMANS, journalist, Amsterdam, Netherlands

BIBIANO F. OSORIO-TAFALL, Director General, Centro de Estudios Económicos y Sociales del Tercer Mundo, Mexico City, Mexico

AURELIO PECCEI, President, The Club of Rome, Rome, Italy

JAMES PERKINS, International Council for Educational Development, New York, USA

MICHEL de PERROT, Groupe de Bellerive, Geneva, Switzerland

RICCARDO PETRELLA, FAST Program, EEC, Brussels, Belgium

VIJAI PILLAI, Center for the Study of Developing Countries, New Delhi, India

JUAN RADA, Centre Européen de Coordination de Recherche et de Documentation en Sciences Sociales, Vienna, Austria (Chile*)

IBRAHIM HELMI ABDEL RAHMAN, Advisor, Cairo, Egypt

MAJID RAHNEMA, Member, executive board, UNESCO, Paris, France (Iran*)

BETTY REARDON, World Council for Curriculum and Instruction, New York, USA

JOHN M. RICHARDSON, American University, Washington, D.C., USA

ANA-MARIA SANDI, Systems Study Division, University of Bucharest, Bucharest, Romania

ADAM SCHAFF, Chairman, Centre Européen de Coordination de Recherche et de Documentation en Sciences Sociales, Vienna, Austria (Poland*)

WOLFGANG SCHUERER, WS Management Consultancy, St. Gallen, Switzerland

FRANZ SEITELBERGER, Institute of Neurophysiology, University of Vienna, Vienna, Austria

ANDRZEJ SICINSKI, "Poland 2000", Polish Academy of Sciences, Warsaw, Poland

KOSON SRISANG, World Council of Churches, Geneva, Switzerland

* Indicates nationality where different from place of work.

N.L.T.L.—L

LUMINITZA STATE, Systems Study Division, University of Bucharest, Bucharest, Romania

JAN STRZELECKI, Institute of Sociology and Philosophy, Warsaw, Poland

BOGDAN SUCHODOLSKI, Academy of Sciences, Warsaw, Poland

PATRICK SUPPES, Stanford University, Stanford, California, USA

CLAUDE MADEMBA SY, Ambassador of the Republic of Senegal, Vienna, Austria

ALEXANDER SZALAI, Hungarian Academy of Social Sciences, Budapest, Hungary

BRUNO TEDESCHI, journalist, *Il Messaggero,* Rome, Italy

SALVATORE TERESI, Center for Lifelong Learning, Paris, France

ALBERT TÉVOÉDJRÈ, Director, International Institute for Labour Studies, Geneva, Switzerland (Benin*)

ROMESH THAPAR, Editor, *Seminar,* New Delhi, India

IBA DER THIAM, University of Dakar, Dakar, Senegal

HUGO THIEMANN, Nestlé, S.A., Vevey, Switzerland

VICTOR URQUIDI, President, El Collegio de Mexico, Mexico City, Mexico

ROBERTO VACCA, writer; member, The Club of Rome, Rome, Italy

DRAGOS VAIDA, Faculty of Mathematics, University of Bucharest, Bucharest, Romania

RENATO VERTUNNI, journalist, RAI-TV, Rome, Italy

HERTA VOMSTEIN, Director, Seminar Center for Economic and Social Development, German Foundation for International Development, Berlin, Federal Republic of Germany

JACQUES VONÈCHE, Jean Piaget Professor of Child and Adult Psychology, University of Geneva, Geneva, Switzerland (Belgium*)

WILLEM H. WELLING, Executive Director, Bernard van Leer Foundation, The Hague, Netherlands

BURNS H. WESTON, Faculty of Law, University of Iowa, Iowa, USA

PATRICK WINSTON, Director, Artificial Intelligence Laboratory, MIT, Cambridge, Mass., USA

EICHI YAMAZAKI, Nichiren Shoshu Française, Sceaux, France

M. ZACHARIEV, UNESCO, Paris, France (Bulgaria*)

* Indicates nationality where different from place of work.

HERBERT ZDARZIL, Department of Education, University of Vienna,
  Vienna, Austria
JOHN ZEISEL, Harvard University, Cambridge, Mass., USA
ABDELWAHED ZHIRI, National Ministry of Education, Rabat,
  Morocco

Index

About the Authors

Dr. Mircea MALITZA has been Romanian Minister of Education from 1970 to 1972 and is now professor at the Faculty of Mathematics at the University of Bucharest. He has lectured on international affairs at academic centers in Geneva, Stockholm, Boston, London, Vienna, Khartoum, New York, and Tokyo. He is a member of the Romanian Academy, of the Union of Writers, and of the Romanian Association for International Law and International Relations. His writings are in the field of education, mathematics, diplomacy, plus various literary essays. His books include *The Chronicle of the Year 2000* and *The Grey Gold* which were translated into several languages. *The Mathematics of Organization* (Abacus Owen, 1974) is available in English.

Dr. James W. BOTKIN is an Associate in Education at the Harvard Graduate School of Education (Cambridge, Mass.) for the duration of the Learning Project. Previously, he was the Academic Director of the Salzburg Seminar in Salzburg, Austria. He received his doctorate in 1973 from the Harvard Business School in the field of higher education management and computer-based systems. His articles have specialized in international affairs, global issues, management, and education. He is presently associated with the International Center for Integrative Studies, 45 West 18th Street, New York, N.Y. 10011.

Dr. Mahdi ELMANDJRA, professor at the University Mohamed V, Rabat has served as Director General of the Moroccan Broadcasting and Television Services, as Counsellor in the Moroccan Mission to the United Nations, and has been for over fifteen years (1961–1976) an international civil servant in UNESCO where he occupied the posts of Chief of the Africa Division, Director of the Executive Office of the Director General, Assistant Director General for Social Sciences and Culture, Assistant Director General for Programming and Special Advisor to the Director General. He is President of the World Future Studies Federation and the author of several publications including *The United Nations System: An Analysis* (Faber & Faber, 1973).

159